I0707308

Trivia Quest

Mastering the Art of Random Knowledge

A Random Walk Down Trivia Lane

Trivia Quest: Mastering the Art of Random Knowledge

A Random Walk Down Trivia Lane

Copyright 2024

Adicus Abbott

The following book of random trivia is for entertainment purposes only. Records and statistics change over time, and were accurate at the time of publication, to the author's best knowledge. Please consult a professional where business, legal, or health matters demand up to the minute accuracy. Enjoy, and get ready to elevate your mastery of random stuff worthy of sharing…or quietly absorbing for yourself.

ISBN: 9798332896460
Independently published

Table of Contents

A Random Walk Down Trivia Lane   7

Pop Culture and Entertainment   9

History and Historical Events   29

Science and Nature Facts   57

Geography and World Facts   77

Literature and Authors   99

Sports and Athletes   117

Music and Music History   129

Film and Television   149

Technology and Innovation   167

Wining and Dining   181

Business and Finance   197

Random Questions and Answers   213

A Random Walk Down Trivia Lane

Two thousand years ago the intersection of three roads in Ancient Rome introduced the world to the lure of trivia.

The word *trivia* is a combination of the words *tri* and *via*, meaning three roads. Long before cell phones, email, radios, and telegraph wires, travelers passed messages and communicated by leaving notes in common areas, in the hopes that somebody would read the note and pass the message on to its intended destination.

One of the most popular areas to leave notes for fellow travelers was at the intersection of three roads north of Rome. Travelers would stop at the intersection and spend hours reading posted notes, essentially gathering random information about other travelers, such as their destination, health, gossip, and well wishes to other friends and family who may pass along.

Over the years this tradition of sharing information at the *Tri Via* intersection came to be known as trivia, feeding the insatiable curiosity of humans everywhere.

It has been said that curiosity killed the cat. But what is often not mentioned is the second line…satisfaction brought him back.

Fortunately, you don't have to be a cat to be curious about the world around you. In fact, curiosity is a typical human trait, and among humans, curiosity is what separates the enlightened from the dullards, and the pub quiz tournament losers from the winners.

So, welcome enlightened one.

Adicus Abbott

Pop Culture and Entertainment

You don't have to wait generations to see changes in pop culture and entertainment. Every day, we are bombarded with fashion changes, new music, upcoming movies, and amazing innovative technological developments that change the ways we communicate, interact, and even amuse ourselves.

Put your shoes on and tighten your laces. We're about to take a totally random walk through a neighborhood called pop culture. We'll start with a stop at the The 27 Club. A club you do not want to join.

The 27 Club is not a real club, and it is not a club you would recommend for a friend or co-worker, or find reviewed on Yelp. In fact, the 27 Club corresponds to musicians and celebrities who died at the age of 27, often due to drug overdoses, alcoholism, or leading a fast and furious lifestyle.

In 1920, Pulitzer Prize winning poet (awarded in 1923) Edna St. Vincent Millay wrote a poem called *First Fig*, where she defended "burning the candle at both ends."

"My candle burns at both ends

It will not last the night;
But ah, my foes, and oh, my friends -
It gives a lovely light."

Members of the 27 Club epitomize burning the candle at both ends.

Notable members of the 27 Club include: Jim Morrison, Pamela Courson (partner to Jim Morrison), Kurt Cobain, Janis Joplin, Jimi Hendrix, and dozens of other artists, writers, musicians, and celebrities.

While the idea of a 27 Club is intriguing, in actuality, statistical evidence suggests the most common age at death for musicians is 56.

As a side note, the 2016 video game called *Hitman* included a mission to kill a musician who was celebrating his 27th birthday.

* * *

Text messages, emails, and comment sections in articles and videos often use abbreviations to make a point or respond to a question. Here are the most common abbreviations you may encounter:

BRB: Be Right Back
BTW: By the Way
OMG: Oh my God
IDK: I Don't Know
TTYL: Talk to You Later
OMW: On My Way
SMH: Shaking My Head
LOL: Laugh Out Loud
TBD: To be Determined
IMHO: In My Humble Opinion

IMO: In My Opinion
OG: Original Gangsters, or Old Guy
FWIW: For What It's Worth
ATM: At the Moment
FOMO: Fear of Missing Out
TLDR: Too Long, Didn't Read
ROTFL: Rolling on the Floor Laughing

Country music stars Faith Hill and Tim McGraw fell in love and married in 1997. They have three children, and as of 2024, remain together.

The 2021 miniseries *1883*, created by Taylor Sheridan, features an amazing cast of Sam Elliott, Tim McGraw, Faith Hill, and Isabel May. McGraw is a very capable guide and freelance soldier type who plays the husband to a strong and gorgeous wife played by Faith Hill. Their daughter, played by Isabel May, is a fiercely independent young woman who embraces the western lifestyle.

The basic story involves a wagon train of German pioneers setting out for Oregon. From 1836 to around 1869, over 400,000 settlers traveled the 2,170 mile Oregon Trail from Missouri to the Willamette Valley in Oregon. The year 1883, portrayed in the miniseries, is late in the Oregon Trail timeline, but the timing fits with the height of the Wild West era.

The shows creator, Taylor Sheridan, rose to stardom as the deputy in the motorcycle crime drama *Sons of Anarchy*, produced between 3 October 2008 and 9 December 2014. Since then, Taylor Sheridan has helped create, write, and direct several hit movies and shows, including: *Wind River*, *Yellowstone*, *Tulsa King*, and *1923*, among others.

Ever heard of cottagecore?

In 2023, "cottagecore" took over social media. People began romanticizing rural life, sharing photos of quaint cabins, homemade bread, and vintage dresses. Even city dwellers joined in, creating cozy corners in their apartments. This trend offered a nostalgic escape from fast-paced, digital-heavy lifestyles, embracing simplicity and nature.

My personal tribute to cottagecore also fits the simpler lifestyle, and is in fact trending now…ditching the smart phone for a flip phone.

In 2024, the unexpected resurgence of roller skating took the world by storm. What started as a few nostalgic posts on TikTok quickly spiraled into a full-blown trend. People of all ages dusted off old skates or bought new ones, flooding parks and boardwalks with vibrant wheels and retro outfits. Skating influencers emerged, showcasing tricks, dances, and even DIY skate customizations. Music from the 70s and 80s, reminiscent of roller disco days, saw a revival as the perfect soundtrack to these skating sessions.

Skate boot factories in China, and the rising star in consumer manufacturing, Vietnam, caught on fast, releasing limited-edition skates and accessories. Celebrities joined in, posting their own skating adventures, further fueling the trend. Roller rinks, once struggling to stay open, saw a boom in business. The trend wasn't just about fun; it symbolized a return to simpler joys and a desire to connect in a physically engaging, nostalgic way. As people glided through streets and parks, they found community, joy, and a bit of freedom on eight wheels.

Personally, I'll consider going roller skating the day skating rinks start issuing hip pads wit their skates. The last thing I need is a fractured hip…thank you very much.

In 2024, "slow fashion" became more than just a buzzword; it transformed into a cultural movement.

Fed up with fast fashion's environmental toll, people began embracing sustainable, high-quality clothing. Thrift stores and vintage shops thrived as consumers sought unique, durable pieces. Social media was flooded with DIY tutorials on upcycling old clothes and tips for building a minimalist wardrobe. Influencers shifted their focus to promoting ethical brands and transparent supply chains.

The movement gained momentum as documentaries and campaigns highlighted fashion's impact on the planet. This shift marked a collective step towards mindful consumption and a more sustainable future.

Incidentally, I've practiced slow fashion for the majority of my life. The only difference in the jeans, shirt, and boots I wear today, versus thirty years ago, is the waist size of my jeans.

In 2024, "digital detox dating" became a fresh trend in the dating scene.

As people grew weary of endless swiping and superficial connections on dating apps, a movement emerged emphasizing offline interactions and deeper, more meaningful connections. Singles began organizing and attending "phone-free" events, where devices were either left at home or checked in at the door. Activities ranged from group hikes and cooking classes to art workshops and book clubs, providing organic settings for genuine interactions. Social media influencers and celebrities started advocating for the trend, sharing their positive experiences and encouraging followers to disconnect to reconnect.

A resurgence in traditional dating practices also followed, with handwritten notes, spontaneous meet-ups, and face-to-face conversations becoming the norm once again. The trend underscored a broader societal yearning for authenticity in an era dominated by digital interactions. By stepping away from screens, people found that love and connection flourished in more natural, unfiltered ways.

I'm so thankful to be above and beyond the dating scene. It's a wonder to me how anybody meets their soulmate today.

•▬▬▬▬• •▬▬▬▬•

Sadfishing is a sad trend online among the social media crowd whereby a person will dramatize his or her emotions, relevant to a real or perceived event, in an attempt to garner sympathy from his or her followers. For example, a person may post, "My dog has to be put to sleep. I'm lost. What do I do?"

Okay, I get it. Pets are family, and putting a loved pet down can be stressful. But a sadfisher may not even own a dog. He or she is fishing for sympathy, even when it is unearned or not even relevant to his or her reality.

Similarly, vague booking is a process of vaguely alluding to being under duress or emotional stress...again, with the intent of collecting likes, views, and sympathy from the online crowd.

Have you ever wondered how long a newly arrived resident of Alaska has to live in Alaska before being given the honorific "sourdough" title?

Traditionally, a new resident to Alaska needs to be in the state for at least 6 months, or have survived one winter, in order to be crowned a sourdough. The sourdough title is complimentary and is given in recognition of the sourdough tradition in Alaska. As a new arrival in Alaska as a high school student, I couldn't wait to earn the sourdough title. Until then, you were just a newbie from the lower, or lesser, 48.

During the gold rush era in Alaska and the Klondike, sourdough bread was considered a survival food. Its popularity in Alaska remains strong to this day.

Another clever word unique to Alaska culture is "Termination Dust."

As I discovered in the fall of my first year in Alaska, termination dust is the first sprinkling of snow on the mountain tops, that has a way of terminating dreams and sending newcomers, especially gold diggers back in the Klondike Gold Rush era, racing for warmer climes. Once winter sets in, a miner could easily find himself trapped in the bush until breakup…which is yet another Alaska word for the melting of the winter ice on the river.

During a recent livestream, popular internet personality Jamie "TechGuru" Lee unboxed the highly anticipated next generation virtual reality (VR) headset, VirtuX Pro. Midway through the stream, Jamie's cat, Pixel, jumped onto the desk, causing the headset to tumble and accidentally activating it. To everyone's surprise, Pixel's movements were perfectly captured in the VR world, creating a hilarious scene of a cat exploring a virtual landscape. The clip went viral almost instantly, with #PixelVR trending worldwide. Fans loved the unexpected crossover of tech and pets, and Jamie capitalized on the moment, releasing a series of Pixel-themed VR content, delighting his audience even more.

Even more telling, is how virtual reality is becoming more prevalent in our lives.

VR is transforming gaming, education, and remote work. It offers immersive experiences, enhances learning, and fosters virtual collaboration. VR's impact on society includes improved training simulations and virtual social interactions, as well as escapism and easy access to simulated engagement and experiences, promising a future where digital and physical realities seamlessly integrate, revolutionizing various industries.

Coachella, an annual music and arts festival held in Indio, California, is a cultural phenomenon that attracts music enthusiasts and celebrities worldwide. Founded in 1999, it has grown into a multi-weekend event, showcasing diverse genres from rock and hip-hop to electronic dance music.

Known for its iconic desert backdrop, Coachella features performances by top-tier artists, emerging talents, and surprise guest appearances. Beyond music, it boasts large-scale art installations, gourmet food vendors, and fashion-forward attendees, making it a trendsetting hub. The festival's influence extends globally, impacting music trends, fashion, and social media, solidifying its status as a premier cultural event.

Building on its reputation for introducing the world to up and coming music and bands, the K-Pop group known as Blackpink performed at Coachella in 2023.

Random Q & A

Question: In the TV show *Breaking Bad*, what is the street name of the blue crystal meth Walter White manufactures?

Answer: Blue Sky.

Question: Who directed the 1994 film *Pulp Fiction*?

Answer: Quentin Tarantino.

Question: Which singer-songwriter released the album *21* in 2011, featuring hits like *Rolling in the Deep* and *Someone Like You*?

Answer: Adele.

Question: What is the name of the fictional continent where most of the action takes place in the TV series *Game of Thrones*?

Answer: Westeros.

Question: Which actress played the character of Hermione Granger in the *Harry Potter* film series?

Answer: Emma Watson.

Question: Who is the creator of the animated TV series *The Simpsons*?

Answer: Matt Groening.

Question: What is the highest-grossing film of all time (as of 2022), surpassing *Avatar*?

Answer: *Avengers: Endgame.*

Question: In the Marvel Cinematic Universe, what is the name of Tony Stark's AI assistant voiced by Paul Bettany?

Answer: J.A.R.V.I.S. (Just A Rather Very Intelligent System).

Question: Which actor portrayed the character of Jack Dawson in the film *Titanic*?

Answer: Leonardo DiCaprio.

Question: What is the real name of the British musician known professionally as "Elton John"?

Answer: Reginald Kenneth Dwight.

Question: Who wrote the novel *The Great Gatsby*, which was adapted into several films, including the 2013 version starring Leonardo DiCaprio?

Answer: F. Scott Fitzgerald.

Question: In the TV series *Friends*, which character famously says, "We were on a break"?

Answer: Ross Geller.

Question: Which actress played the role of Katniss Everdeen in the film adaptations of *The Hunger Games* series?

Answer: Jennifer Lawrence.

Question: What is the name of the fictional paper company featured in the American version of the TV show *The Office*?

Answer: Dunder Mifflin.

Question: Which rock band released the album *Abbey Road* in 1969?

Answer: The Beatles.

Question: Who is the author of the *Harry Potter* book series?

Answer: J.K. Rowling.

Question: Which actor portrayed the character of Neo in the film *The Matrix*?

Answer: Keanu Reeves.

Question: What is the name of the fictional land in the animated film *Frozen* where Elsa and Anna reside?

Answer: Arendelle.

Question: Who played the character of Tyler Durden in the cult classic film *Fight Club*?

Answer: Brad Pitt.

Question: In the TV show *Stranger Things*, what is the name of the alternate dimension that is home to the Demogorgon?

Answer: The Upside Down.

Question: Tom Holland, a British actor famous for his portrayal of Spider Man in various *Avenger* remakes of the movie franchise once performed on *Lip Sync Battle*. What song did he perform?

Answer: *Umbrella*. A song released by Rihanna on March 29, 2007.

Question: Speaking of Rihanna, what is her real name?

Answer: Robyn Fenty.

Question: Although she is better known for singing, Taylor Swift made her acting debut in which movie?

Answer: *Valentine's Day*. The movie was released in 2010 and is set in Los Angeles. As the title suggests, the movie is about the pressures and expectations couples encounter on Valentine's Day.

Question: Lady Gaga is known as the godmother of what famous singer's children?

Answer: Elton John.

Question: Which actor voiced the character of Woody in the *Toy Story* series?

Answer: Tom Hanks

Question: What is the name of the first studio album released by Taylor Swift?

Answer: *Taylor Swift.*

Question: Who played the role of Jack Dawson in the movie *Titanic*?

Answer: Leonardo DiCaprio.

Question: Which band released the song *Bohemian Rhapsody* in 1975?

Answer: Queen.

Question: In which year did the first *Harry Potter* movie come out?

Answer: 2001.

Question: What was the name of the song by Pharrell Williams that became a huge hit in 2013 and was featured in the movie *Despicable Me 2*?

Answer: *Happy*.

Question: Which celebrity is known for the hit song *Just the Way You Are* released in 2010?

Answer: Bruno Mars.

Question: Who directed the movie *E.T. The Extra-Terrestrial*?

Answer: Steven Spielberg.

Question: Which famous pop star's real name is Stefani Joanne Angelina Germanotta?

Answer: Lady Gaga.

Question: Who played the role of Wolverine in the *X-Men* series?

Answer: Hugh Jackman.

Question: Which movie features the famous quote, "You can't handle the truth!"?

Answer: *A Few Good Men*. Statement was made by actor Jack Nicholson during a pivotal point in his character's court martial.

Question: Who is the lead singer of the band Coldplay?

Answer: Chris Martin.

Question: What is the name of the debut single of Billie Eilish released in 2015?

Answer: *Ocean Eyes.*

Question: Which actor starred as Tony Stark in the *Marvel Cinematic Universe*?

Answer: Robert Downey Jr.

Question: Which 1994 film won the Academy Award for Best Picture and stars Tom Hanks as the lead character?

Answer: *Forrest Gump.*

Question: What is the name of Beyoncé's 2016 visual album?

Answer: *Lemonade.*

Question: Who played the role of Joker in the 2019 film Joker?

Answer: Joaquin Phoenix. Heath Ledger played the Joker in the 2008 release of *The Dark Knight.*

Question: Which actor is known for playing Deadpool in the Marvel movies?

Answer: Ryan Reynolds.

Question: In which year was Michael Jackson's album *Thriller* released?

Answer: 1982.

Question: Who directed the *Lord of the Rings* trilogy?

Answer: Peter Jackson.

Question: What song did Whitney Houston famously cover in 1992 for the film *The Bodyguard*?

Answer: *I Will Always Love You.*

Question: Which actress won an Oscar for her role in the 2010 film *Black Swan*?

Answer: Natalie Portman.

Question: What is the title of Ed Sheeran's 2017 hit song that was number one in multiple countries?

Answer: *Shape of You.*

Question: Who played the character of Hermione Granger in the Harry Potter series?

Answer: Emma Watson. Emma Charlotte Duerre Watson was 11 years old when *Harry Potter and the Philosopher's Stone* was released in November 2001.

Question: Which artist released the hit song "Flowers" in 2023?

Answer: Miley Cyrus.

Question: What TV show had its final season air in 2023, ending a 10-year run?

Answer: "The Walking Dead."

Question: Who won the Grammy for Album of the Year in 2023?

Answer: Harry Styles for "Harry's House."

Question: Which video game won the Game of the Year award at The Game Awards 2023?

Answer: "The Legend of Zelda: Tears of the Kingdom."

Question: What is the name of the latest Marvel Cinematic Universe film released in 2024?

Answer: "Captain America: Brave New World."

Question: Which celebrity broke the record for the most followers on Instagram in 2023?

Answer: Cristiano Ronaldo.

Question: What streaming service premiered the hit series "Wednesday" in 2022?

Answer: Netflix.

Question: Who played the lead role in the 2023 blockbuster "Oppenheimer"?

Answer: Cillian Murphy.

Question: What animated film won the Oscar for Best Animated Feature in 2023?

Answer: "Guillermo del Toro's Pinocchio."

Question: Who hosted the 2023 Oscars?

Answer: Jimmy Kimmel.

Question: Which actor starred as Mario in the 2023 animated film "The Super Mario Bros. Movie"?

Answer: Chris Pratt.

Question: What book series adaptation became a hit TV show on Amazon Prime in 2023?

Answer: "The Wheel of Time."

Question: What popular podcast was adapted into a TV series on HBO in 2023?

Answer: "The Last Podcast on the Left."

Question: Which actress won an Emmy for her role in "Euphoria" in 2023?

Answer: Zendaya.

Question: What is the name of Taylor Swift's 2023 re-recorded album?

Answer: "Speak Now (Taylor's Version)."

Question: Who directed the 2023 film "Barbie"?

Answer: Greta Gerwig.

Question: Which social media platform introduced a new feature called "Threads" in 2023?

Answer: Instagram.

History and Historical Events

History is the study of past events, particularly those events involving people, nations, governments, and wars. Historians study artifacts, as well as written and oral records to construct narratives, or interpret past events.

The study of history is important in terms of helping future generations understand past events, and how those events impacted people and cultures. An old adage suggests those who fail to learn history are doomed to repeat it. The original source for this adage has been attributed to philosophers George Santayana and Edmund Burke, as well as various politicians, including Winston Churchill.

The closest written record of this adage is attributed to George Santayana in his book, *The Life of Reason, or The Phases of Human Progress*, published in 1905.

While historical trivia hardly scratches the depth of the human experience, it does offer a starting point in understanding who we are, and where we have been. In that regard, the study of generations offers a compelling glimpse into the history of humans.

A generation is a group of people born in roughly the same time period. In America, we like to define people born within a 13-30 year time span as a specific generation.

The study of populations and generations is known as demography. Amazingly, the cultural norms, circumstances, and events of each generation impacts a person's values and personality, and makes generalizations about the traits of each generation fairly accurate.

Check out the latest generation names and traits below.

The Greatest Generation is made up of the people who lived through the Depression and fought in the Second World War. They created jazz and swing music and were known for their strong work ethic and grit. Demographers define the Greatest Generation as anyone born between 1901 and 1927.

The Silent Generation was born between the years 1928 and 1945. They were children during the Depression and came of age during the Second World War. They were known as conformists, perhaps from years of struggling to survive in hard economic times, as well as a devastating war when over 12 million men and women were deployed to fight against Nazi Germany and Imperial Japan.

Baby Boomers represent the largest portion of the U.S. population, and are named for the surge of babies born after the Second World War. Demographers define the Boomers generation as anyone born from 1946 to 1964. They are known as a rebellious generation, who gave rise to the hippie movement, war protests, and the broad acceptance of Rock and Roll music.

Generation X, also known as the "Slacker Generation," represents those born between 1965 and 1980. Despite their reputation for slacking, this generation represents devotion to family, and their children's education. They came of age during the disco era and laid the groundwork for the 1980s.

The Millennials were born between the years 1981 and 1996. This generation witnessed 9/11 as children, and saw the rise of the Internet. And while they can remember the birth of Amazon, they also quickly adapted to the innovation of cell phones, and posting videos on You Tube. In short, this generation loves technology and environmental activism.

Generation Z represents people born between the years 1997 and 2010. This generation never knew a world without connectivity. They are comfortable with technology, and spend a lot of time in front of screens…such as phones, computers, and video games. However, this generation should not be underestimated. They are highly aware of politics, inclusion, and environmental activism.

Generation Alpha represents people born between the years 2011 and 2024. They live comfortably in a world dominated by social media and may be considered the most technologically inclined generation of them all. While Boomers may have witnessed the Moon landings, this generation will see manned missions to Mars and beyond, and rather than marvel at the great leaps of mankind, they will take it as a given. Sadly, they are also coming of age in a time when worldwide pandemics are expected, and most grow up in single parent households.

Americans celebrate their date of independence on the 4th of July. However, Congress voted to declare independence from British colonial rule on 2 July 1776. The Declaration of

Independence was ratified by Congress on 4 July 1776. The document was actually signed by the delegates on 2 August 1776.

Portraits and various artist depictions of Congress meeting in Philadelphia creates a deceptive image. In actuality, all the members of Congress rarely met at the same time. In fact, on many occasions they barely had more than a handful of delegates in attendance. This was not the result of lack of enthusiasm, but a necessity. Their meetings were held in secret, and all the delegates were part time statesman. They all had farms or businesses to tend.

Portraits of the time also create the image that our Founding Fathers were elder statesman. In fact, on 4 July 1776, many of the delegates were in their 30s and 40s. Notably, James Monroe was 18, Aaron Burr was 20, Alexander Hamilton was 21, and James Madison was 25.

Virtually every child in America was taught a lesson in morality and honesty during elementary school using a story of George Washington as a child admitting to his father that he chopped down the cherry tree. To reinforce the morality lesson, Washington reportedly stated, "I cannot tell a lie."

But did it ever happen? Or was this just a case of parents, teachers, civic leaders, and church leaders creating a lie to teach children not to lie?

A minister and bookseller named Mason Locke Weems wrote a book called The Life of Washington shortly after Washington's death in 1799. Weems stated his objective was to teach children that greatness can be obtained by leading a virtuous life. The first four editions of his popular book did not include the cherry tree story, however, by 1806, the story of the cherry tree and Washington's admission of guilt became part of the historical record. There is no evidence, outside of the author's book, to suggest the cherry tree story is true.

The Industrial Revolution, which began in Britain in the late 1800s changed life as we know it. It was a period of profound technological, economic, and social change. It marked the transition from agrarian economies to industrialized and urban ones.

Innovations such as the steam engine, spinning jenny, and power loom revolutionized manufacturing processes, leading to mass production and the rise of factories. This era saw significant advancements in transportation, including railways and steamships, facilitating trade and mobility.

The Industrial Revolution also brought about significant social changes, including urbanization, shifts in labor patterns, and the growth of a new industrial working class.

The signing of the Magna Carta in 1215 was a landmark event in world history that profoundly impacted the development of modern democratic principles.

Facing a rebellion from his barons due to oppressive taxation and arbitrary justice, King John of England was compelled to affix his seal to this "Great Charter." The Magna Carta established the principle that everyone, including the king, was subject to the law. It guaranteed rights to a fair trial and protection from unlawful imprisonment, laying the groundwork for individual liberties.

Though initially intended to address feudal grievances, its broader implications resonated through centuries, influencing the constitutional frameworks of numerous countries, including the United States. The Magna Carta's legacy is its enduring assertion of the rule of law and the idea that justice should be accessible to all.

This historic document remains a symbol of the fight against tyranny and the pursuit of human rights and democracy.

The Berlin Conference of 1884-1885 was a defining moment in the imperial colonization of Africa, shaping the continent's political landscape for decades to come. Convened by German Chancellor Otto von Bismarck, the conference brought together major European powers to negotiate and formalize their territorial claims in Africa, a process that became known as the "Scramble for Africa."

Without any African representatives present, the attendees drew arbitrary borders, disregarding existing ethnic, cultural, and linguistic boundaries.

The agreements reached at the Berlin Conference accelerated the colonization of Africa, leading to the exploitation of its resources and people. European powers established colonies, extracting raw materials to fuel their industrial economies while imposing foreign governance structures. This period of imperial colonization had lasting impacts, including the disruption of traditional societies, economic exploitation, and the introduction of European cultural and political systems.

The legacy of the Berlin Conference and subsequent colonization continues to influence Africa's political and social dynamics to this day.

The First Fleet's arrival in Botany Bay on January 26, 1788, marks a pivotal event in Australian history, establishing the foundation for modern Australia. Commanded by Captain Arthur Phillip, the fleet comprised eleven ships carrying over 1,000 convicts, marines, and officials from Britain, sent to establish a penal colony. This expedition, driven by Britain's need to alleviate overcrowded prisons, led to the creation of the first European settlement in Australia at Sydney Cove.

The settlement faced immediate challenges, including harsh environmental conditions, limited supplies, and conflicts with Indigenous peoples, whose land and way of life were profoundly disrupted. Despite these hardships, the colony gradually expanded, laying the groundwork for further exploration and colonization of the continent.

The arrival of the First Fleet initiated significant demographic, social, and cultural transformations, influencing Australia's development into a diverse and prosperous nation. This event is commemorated annually as Australia Day, reflecting on both the nation's achievements and the enduring impact on Indigenous communities.

The Korean War, erupting in 1950, stemmed from Cold War tensions and Korea's division after World War II. North Korea, backed by the Soviet Union and China, invaded South Korea, supported by the United Nations and primarily the United States. This conflict highlighted ideological rivalries and geopolitical ambitions, becoming a proxy war that shaped the post-war order in East Asia.

Often referred to as the "Forgotten War," over 3 million people died in the war, including over 53,000 U.S. service members. Technically, there is a cease fire agreement in effect between North and South Korea. However, a state of war still exists.

Random Q & A

Question: When did the United States Post Office first start using postage stamps?

Answer: The Post Office issued its first postage stamps on 1 July 1847. It offered two denominations, a five cent stamp, and a ten cent stamp. A portrait of Benjamin Franklin was used for the five cent stamp, with George Washington on the ten cent stamp. Interestingly, the stamps were printed on non-perforated sheets. The postal clerk used scissors to cut each stamp from the sheet as it was purchased.

Question: What is the name of the German zeppelin that crashed at Lakehurst Naval Air Station in New Jersey on 6 May 1937?

Answer: The Hindenburg. More than 30 people died in the accident, essentially ending the use of dirigibles, or blimps, as commercial air travel. Similar aircraft, such as the Goodyear blimp, are only used for advertising and aerial views of sporting events.

Question: What was the last state to join the United States?

Answer: Hawaii became the 50th state on 21 August 1959. Alaska preceded Hawaii on 3 January 1959, and is known as the 49th State.

While there are currently 50 recognized states in the United States, there are also 14 territories attached to the United States. Of those, five are inhabited: American Samoa, Guam, Northern Mariana Islands, Puerto Rico, and the United States Virgin Islands. The nine uninhabited territories include various small islands and atolls in the South Pacific.

Question: What year did the Russian Revolution occur?

Answer: 1917.

Question: What was the primary purpose of the Great Wall of China?

Answer: To protect against invasions from northern tribes.

Question: Thomas Jefferson is credited with writing the first draft of the Declaration of Independence? However, during the formative years of the United States, Alexander Hamilton, James Madison, and John Jay compiled a series of essays promoting the creation of a constitution. What was the name of their book?

Answer: The Federalist Papers.

Question: What is the actual "birthdate" of the United States?

Answer:
Question: Who was the first female Prime Minister of the United Kingdom?

Answer: Margaret Thatcher. Ms. Thatcher was known as a very strong willed person, and had the nickname, The Iron Lady. She and President Ronald Reagan were good friends.

If you get a chance, look her up online. There are videos available showing her debating in Parliament.

Question: Who was the first President of South Africa after the end of apartheid?

Answer: Nelson Mandela. Apartheid in South Africa was a policy that governed relations between South Africa's white minority and nonwhite majority. Apartheid sanctioned racial segregation and political and economic discrimination based on skin color. South Africa phased out its apartheid policies in the early 1990s.

Question: Who was the first African American Supreme Court Justice?

Answer: Thurgood Marshall. Marshall served on the Supreme Court from 1967 to 1991.

Question: In what year did women gain the right to vote in the United States?

Answer: 1920. The right to vote is known as suffrage. Women protested and advocated for change in the voting laws in America for over 100 years before finally winning their right to vote on 18 Auguast 1920 when the 19th Amendment to the Constitution was ratified, granting women in America the right to vote.

Question: Which amendment to the Constitution abolished slavery?

Answer: The 13th Amendment. However, prior to ratification of the 13th Amendment, Abraham Lincoln's Executive Order, known as the Emancipation Proclamation, went into effect.

One of the newest holidays on the American official holiday calendar is Juneteenth. Juneteenth celebrates the announcement of the end of slavery. Technically, 19 June 1865 was the day Texas recognized the Emancipation Proclamation.

Question: What year did the United States land the first man on the moon?

Answer: 1969. On 20 July 1969, Astronauts Neil Armstrong and Buzz Aldrin became the first human beings to walk on the Moon. Their Apollo 11 Lunar Module, named Eagle, landed in an area known as the Sea of Tranquility. Upon landing, the first transmission from Armstrong was, "Houston, Tranquility Base here. The Eagle has landed." Amazingly. Armstrong took manual control of the Lunar Module as it approached its landing on the Moon's surface because the landing spot was rocky. By the time Armstrong repositioned the craft and landed it, the Lunar Module had only seconds of fuel left.

Cooler heads prevailed that day, apparently validating NASA's determination to use test pilots as astronauts.

Question: What territory did the U.S. purchase from France in 1803?

Answer: The Louisiana Territory. The 1803 Louisiana Purchase was a huge event in American history, in which the United States acquired approximately 828,000 square miles of territory from France. The deal was struck between U.S. President Thomas Jefferson and French leader Napoleon Bonaparte. The purchase price was $15 million, roughly four cents per acre, effectively doubling the size of the United States and paving the way for westward expansion.

Question: Who discovered penicillin?

Answer: Alexander Fleming.

Question: What was the name of the ship that Christopher Columbus sailed on his first voyage to the Americas?

Answer: The Santa Maria.

Question: Who was the first Emperor of Rome?

Answer: Augustus Caesar.

Question: Which U.S. President purchased Alaska from Russia?

Answer: In 1867, U.S. President Andrew Johnson's administration, under Secretary of State William H. Seward, purchased Alaska from Russia for $7.2 million. Known as "Seward's Folly" due to initial public skepticism, the acquisition added approximately 586,000 square miles of territory to the

United States. The purchase was motivated by the strategic desire to expand American territory, access natural resources, and reduce Russian presence in North America. Over time, Alaska proved valuable for its abundant natural resources, including gold, oil, and fish. The acquisition is now seen as a significant and strategic expansion of U.S. territory.

Question: What was the primary focus of the New Deal programs?

Answer: The New Deal was a series of programs and iniatives to revive the Americn economy and help people find jobs during the Great Depression in the 1930s. President Franklin Roosevelt created federal jobs programs, as well as the Social Security Adminstration under the New Deal.

Question: What was the first state to ratify the U.S. Constitution?

Answer: Delaware ratified the Constitution on 7 December 1787, earning the nickname, First State.

Question: What landmark Supreme Court case ended racial segregation in public schools?

Answer: Brown v. Board of Education (1954) was a landmark Supreme Court ruling that declared racial segregation in public schools unconstitutional. The unanimous decision overturned the "separate but equal" doctrine established by Plessy v. Ferguson (1896), stating that segregated schools were inherently unequal and violated the Equal Protection Clause of the 14th Amendment. This historic ruling was a significant victory for the Civil Rights Movement, paving the way for desegregation and greater racial equality in the United States.

Question: Who was the U.S. President during the majority of the Great Depression?

Answer: Franklin D. Roosevelt.

Question: What was the main purpose of the Lewis and Clark Expedition?

Answer: To explore and map the Louisiana Purchase.

Question: Who was the President of the Confederate States during the Civil War?

Answer: Jefferson Davis.

Question: In what year was the U.S. Constitution ratified?

Answer: 1788.

Question: Who was the first Secretary of the Treasury?

Answer: Alexander Hamilton. Born in the West Indies, he became an aide to George Washington during the Revolutionary War. Hamilton was a key author of the Federalist Papers, advocating for the Constitution. As the first Secretary of the Treasury, he established the national banking system. His political rivalry with Aaron Burr culminated in a fatal duel in 1804.

Question: Who wrote the influential pamphlet "Common Sense" advocating for American independence?

Answer: Thomas Paine.

Thomas Paine (1737-1809) was an influential English-American writer and political activist. His pamphlet "Common Sense" (1776) galvanized colonial support for American independence from Britain. Paine also wrote "The American Crisis," bolstering Revolutionary morale, and "The Rights of Man," defending the French Revolution. His work "The Age of Reason" advocated deism and criticized organized religion. Paine's radical ideas and compelling prose significantly shaped revolutionary thought in both America and Europe.

And just so you'll know, deism is a philosophical belief that suggests the existence of a supreme being who created the universe but does not interfere with its functioning through miracles or supernatural events. Deists believe that this creator set the natural laws in motion and allows the universe to operate according to these laws without further divine intervention. This belief system emerged during the Enlightenment, emphasizing reason, observation, and the study of the natural world as the primary sources of knowledge about the creator, rather than relying on religious texts or doctrines.

Question: What was the name of the ship that brought the Pilgrims to America in 1620?

Answer: The Mayflower.

Question: Who was the U.S. President during the Cuban Missile Crisis?

Answer: John F. Kennedy.

Question: Who led the American forces to victory at the Battle of New Orleans during the War of 1812?

Answer: Andrew Jackson.

Question: What was the primary goal of the Seneca Falls Convention in 1848?

Answer: The Seneca Falls Convention, held in July 1848 in Seneca Falls, New York, was the first women's rights convention in the United States. Organized by Elizabeth Cady Stanton and Lucretia Mott, it gathered around 300 attendees, including both women and men, to discuss the social, civil, and religious rights of women. The convention produced the Declaration of Sentiments, modeled after the Declaration of Independence, which called for equal rights for women, including the right to vote.

This event marked the beginning of the women's suffrage movement in the U.S., setting the stage for future advocacy and legal reforms.

Question: Which U.S. state was an independent republic before joining the Union?

Answer: Texas.

If you've ever heard the expression, "Six flags over Texas," this is what it means: "Six Flags Over Texas" refers to the six different nations that have governed Texas throughout its history. These flags represent Spain, France, Mexico, the

Republic of Texas, the Confederate States of America, and the United States of America. The term is famously associated with the amusement park "Six Flags Over Texas," which opened in 1961 in Arlington, Texas, and was named to reflect this historical heritage. The park features themes and attractions inspired by these six periods of Texan history.

Question: Who was the first woman to run for President of the United States?

Answer: Victoria Woodhull.

Question: What significant event took place on April 14, 1865?

Answer: The assassination of Abraham Lincoln

Question: Which U.S. President signed the Civil Rights Act of 1964?

Answer: Lyndon B. Johnson.

Question: What was the first permanent English settlement in America?

Answer: Jamestown, Virginia.

Question: What was the main objective of the Marshall Plan after World War II?

Answer: To rebuild and aid Western Europe's economies. The Marshall Plan, officially known as the European Recovery

Program, got its name from George C. Marshall, who was the U.S. Secretary of State at the time the plan was proposed. In a speech at Harvard University on June 5, 1947, Marshall outlined the need for a comprehensive program to help rebuild war-torn Europe after World War II. His advocacy and the plan's subsequent implementation led to its association with his name. The Marshall Plan aimed to provide economic assistance to help restore the economies of Western European countries, prevent the spread of communism, and foster political stability.

Question: Who was the Chief Justice of the Supreme Court who presided over the Dred Scott case?

Answer: Roger B. Taney.

Question: Who was the founder of the Persian Empire?

Answer: Cyrus the Great.

Question: What was the main outcome of the Battle of Waterloo?

Answer: The defeat of Napoleon Bonaparte.

Question: Who was the first Secretary-General of the United Nations?

Answer: Trygve Lie (1896-1968) was a Norwegian politician and diplomat who served as the first Secretary-General of the United Nations from 1946 to 1952. He played a crucial role in establishing the UN's foundational structures and promoting international cooperation in the post-World War II era. Lie's tenure faced challenges, including the early Cold War tensions, but he laid the groundwork for the UN's future peacekeeping and humanitarian efforts.

Question: What event sparked the start of the American Revolution?

Answer: The Battles of Lexington and Concord.

Question: Who was the U.S. President during the Louisiana Purchase?

Answer: Thomas Jefferson.

Question: What significant event occurred on July 20, 1969?

Answer: The Apollo 11 moon landing.

Question: Who was the first American woman in space?

Answer: Sally Ride.

Sally Ride (1951-2012) was an American astronaut and physicist, celebrated as the first American woman to travel into space. She flew aboard the Space Shuttle Challenger in 1983. A trailblazer for women in STEM, Ride later became a professor, author, and advocate for science education. Her pioneering achievements and dedication to inspiring future generations have left an enduring legacy in space exploration and science education.

STEM is an educational initiative that emphasizes teaching kids science, technology, engineering, and math.

Question: What was the main purpose of the Monroe Doctrine?

Answer: To prevent European colonization in the Americas. While Manifest Destiny was the belief that the United States should control North America, south of Canada, from coast to coast, in contrast, the Monroe Doctrine believed the United States should have dominion, or at least political control, over the entire Western Hemisphere, including Central America and South America.

Question: Who was the U.S. President during the signing of the Treaty of Versailles?

Answer: Woodrow Wilson.

The Treaty of Versailles (1919) ended World War I, imposing harsh penalties on Germany, including significant territorial losses, military restrictions, and hefty reparations. The treaty's punitive measures led to widespread economic hardship and national humiliation in Germany. This created fertile ground for political instability and resentment. Adolf Hitler and the Nazi Party exploited these conditions, using nationalist rhetoric to rally support. The treaty's failure to foster lasting peace contributed directly to the rise of Hitler and the outbreak of World War II.

Question: What was the primary reason for the Boston Tea Party?

Answer: Protest against British taxation.

Question: Who was the leader of the Soviet Union during the Cuban Missile Crisis?

Answer: Nikita Khrushchev.

Question: In which year did the U.S. enter World War I?

Answer: 1917. the war ended shortly thereafter, on 11 November 1918.

Question: Who was the famous nurse known as the "Lady with the Lamp" during the Crimean War?

Answer: Florence Nightingale.

Question: Which American city was the first to host the Olympic Games?

Answer: St. Louis in 1904.

1904 was a busy year for St. Louis. The St. Louis World's Fair, also known as the Louisiana Purchase Exposition, took place in 1904 to commemorate the centennial of the Louisiana Purchase. It showcased technological innovations, cultural exhibits, and amusements from around the world. The fair introduced new inventions like the ice cream cone and showcased advances in electricity. It attracted millions of visitors and promoted international cooperation, leaving a lasting impact on American culture and industry in the early 20th century.

Question: Who was the U.S. President during the signing of the Camp David Accords?

Answer: Jimmy Carter

Question: What did the Homestead Act of 1862 provide?

Answer: Free land to settlers in the West

The Homestead Act of 1862 was a U.S. law that provided settlers with 160 acres of public land in exchange for a small fee and a commitment to improve the land. It aimed to encourage westward expansion and settlement of the American frontier by granting individuals the opportunity to own land. This legislation accelerated the development of agriculture and settlement in the Midwest and Western United States, shaping the country's demographic and economic landscape.

Question: Who was the first President to live in the White House?

Answer: John Adams.

Question: What was the main cause of the Thirty Years' War?

Answer: Religious conflict between Catholics and Protestants.

The Thirty Years' War (1618-1648) was a devastating conflict primarily fought in Central Europe. It began as a religious war between Protestants and Catholics but evolved into a broader struggle for political power and territory. The war's impact on European politics and society was profound, leading to widespread devastation and population loss.

Question: Who was the famous Greek philosopher who tutored Alexander the Great?

Answer: Aristotle.

Question: In which year did the Korean War begin?

Answer: 1950.

Question: What was the main purpose of the Roman aqueducts?

Answer: To transport water to cities. While not proven, some historians believe the use of lead pipes to distribute water to fountains throughout Rome may have caused lead poisoning among the populace, contributing to the eventual fall of the Roman Empire.

Question: Who was the leader of the Underground Railroad?

Answer: Harriet Tubman.

Question: What was the main cause of World War I?

Answer: The assassination of Archduke Franz Ferdinand

Question: Who was the leader of the Soviet Union during World War II?

Answer: Joseph Stalin.

Question: In what year did the Berlin Wall fall?

Answer: 1989.

The Berlin Wall, erected in 1961 by East Germany to stem emigration to the West, became a symbol of Cold War division. Its fall on November 9, 1989, marked a historic moment as East German authorities unexpectedly opened the border, allowing jubilant crowds to reunite with family and friends in West Berlin. This event catalyzed the reunification of Germany and symbolized the end of communist rule in Eastern Europe, contributing to the Cold War's conclusion.

In the 1962 novel, The Lilies of the Field, by William Edmund Barrett, the nuns struggling to build a chapel in the rural American Southwest, were refugees from East Germany, who escaped by crossing the Berlin Wall at a time when people attempting to escape East Germany were routinely shot.

Question: Who was the first person to circumnavigate the globe?

Answer: Ferdinand Magellan.

Question: Who was the principal author of the Communist Manifesto?

Answer: Karl Marx.

Question: What was the purpose of the Magna Carta?

Answer: To limit the powers of the king and establish certain legal rights.

Question: What was the main goal of the Crusades?

Answer: To capture the Holy Land from Muslim control.

Question: What year did the Titanic sink?

Answer: 1912.

Question: Who was the famous queen of ancient Egypt known for her beauty and diplomatic skills?

Answer: Cleopatra.

Question: What was the main cause of the French Revolution?

Answer: Economic crisis and social inequality.

Question: Who wrote the famous book of philosophy, known as "The Republic.?"

Answer: Plato.

Plato may best be remembered for his Allegory of the Cave, used to explain our understanding of the world. In the allegory, Plato describes a group of people who have lived chained inside a cave since birth, facing a wall and unable to see anything except shadows cast by objects behind them. These shadows are their reality. When one prisoner is freed and emerges from the cave, they are initially blinded by the sunlight but gradually come to see the outside world and realize the true nature of reality. This allegory symbolizes Plato's theory of Forms, where the cave represents the material world of appearances and shadows, while the outside world represents the world of Forms or Ideas—the eternal and immutable truths that are the true reality. It also illustrates Plato's belief in the role of philosophy and education in enlightening individuals and freeing them from ignorance.

Question: In what year did India gain independence from British rule?

Answer: 1947.

Question: Who was the founder of the Mongol Empire?

Answer: Genghis Khan.

Question: What ancient city is known for its extensive library and center of learning?

Answer: Alexandria.

Question: What was the main reason for the outbreak of the Peloponnesian War?

Answer: Rivalry between Athens and Sparta.

Question: What was the primary goal of the Renaissance?

Answer: A revival of art, culture, and learning based on classical antiquity.

Question: Who was the last Tsar of Russia?

Answer: Nicholas II.

Question: In which year did the Battle of Hastings take place?

Answer: 1066.

The Battle of Hastings in 1066 was a pivotal conflict between Norman invaders, led by William the Conqueror, and Anglo-Saxon defenders under King Harold II of England. The Normans triumphed, leading to William's coronation as king and the Norman conquest of England, reshaping English history and culture.

Question: Who was the leader of the Indian independence movement?

Answer: Mahatma Gandhi.

Question: What was the main purpose of the Spanish Inquisition?

Answer: To enforce Catholic orthodoxy and root out heresy.

Question: Who was the famous Carthaginian general who crossed the Alps to invade Rome?

Answer: Hannibal.

Hannibal's invasion of Rome during the Second Punic War (218-201 BC) was a daring military campaign led by the Carthaginian general across the Alps with war elephants. His forces inflicted devastating defeats on Roman armies at battles like Cannae (216 BC). Despite these victories, logistical challenges and lack of reinforcements prevented Hannibal from capturing Rome itself, leading to his eventual withdrawal from Italy by 203 BC.

Question: What ancient civilization is known for creating the first known code of laws, known as the Code of Hammurabi?

Answer: The Babylonians.

The Code of Hammurabi is one of the earliest known written legal codes, dating back to ancient Mesopotamia around 1754 BC. It was established by King Hammurabi of Babylon and consists of 282 laws covering various aspects of society, including crime, commerce, marriage, and property. The code is famous for its principle of "an eye for an eye" and reflects the societal norms and justice system of ancient Babylonian civilization.

Science and Nature Facts

From the microscopic realms of quantum physics to the colossal forces driving weather patterns, science reveals the deep intricacies of our universe. But we won't be going there.

Instead, we'll take a more pedestrian, circuitous, and random walk down triva lane and see what turns up in the world of science and nature. For starts, having just reread Arthur C. Clarke's *2001: A Space Odyssey*, let's talk about the moons of Jupiter.

On 7 January 1610, an Italian astronomer named Galileo Galilei used a homemade 20x power telescope to study the planet Jupiter.

During his observations, he noticed four points of light, which he initially believed were stars, near the planet. Further investigation revealed the points of light were moons, orbiting around Jupiter. These moons came to be known as the Galilean moons, which a German astronomer named German astronomer, Johannes Kepler, named: Io, Europa, Ganymede, and Callisto.

In March of that year, Galileo published his findings in a book called, *Siderius Nuncius.* As of 23 October 2023, scientists know of 95 satellites, or moons, orbiting Jupiter. This number does not include an indetrminant number of moonlets measuring from a meter to a kilometer in diameter.

Ganymede is the largest moon in the solar system, and is even larger than the planet Mercury at a radius of 1,650 miles, which is a measurement from the center of Ganymede to its outer crust.

Scientists also believe the Ganymede surface is covered in a thick icy crust, with an ocean below. If that's true, there is more water on Ganymede than on Earth.

Jupiter is 5.2 times further from the Sun than Earth, or 5.2 astronomical units. It takes sunlight 43 minutes to travel from the Sun to Jupiter.

The average human gets 2 colds per year. It sounds bad, but there are over 200 known viruses floating around that can cause colds. Thanks to our immune system, we can manage to fight off most viral infections.

In the War of the Worlds story by H.G. Wells, the aliens die in their attempt to colonize Earth because they have not adapted to our unique brand of viruses. To paraphrase Wells, the aliens had not earned their right, through thousands of years of evolution, to live on Earth.

An emperor penguin can grow to 4 feet in height. An extinct variety of penguin, known as the colossus penguin, grew to over 6 feet.

African buffaloes vote, and it's the females doing the voting. Buffalo vote by facing the direction they want the herd to move. Which ever direction has the most votes is the direction the herd moves. Does that mean they can also count? After all, what's the use of voting if the votes aren't counted?

In the world of science, anomalies are like mysterious puzzles waiting to be solved. An anomaly is something that doesn't fit the usual pattern or expectation. Imagine if, in a class of identical twins, one suddenly had blue hair! Scientists study anomalies because they can reveal new discoveries about how things work. For example, finding a plant thriving in a desert where no plants should grow teaches us about resilience. These anomalies challenge scientists to think differently and ask new questions. By understanding anomalies, scientists unlock secrets that help us understand our world better.

For example, in Antarctica, scientists have recently discovered a 'hotspot' beneath the ice, where temperatures are unusually warm. This anomaly puzzles researchers because Antarctica is known for extreme cold. Understanding this anomaly could reveal new insights into the stability of ice sheets and climate change.

Black holes are mysterious objects in space where gravity is incredibly strong. They form when massive stars collapse under their own weight. Nothing, not even light, can escape their pull, making them invisible to telescopes. Scientists study them using indirect methods, like watching how nearby stars move. Black holes teach us about the universe's extreme conditions and how gravity affects everything around us. While they seem like cosmic vacuum cleaners, they play a crucial role in shaping galaxies and the cosmos. Understanding them helps us unravel the secrets of space and time.

Black holes are not common in the sense that they are abundant everywhere, but they are widespread in the universe. They form from the remnants of massive stars that collapse under their own gravity. While there are many black holes in our galaxy, the Milky Way, estimates suggest there could be millions to billions of them scattered throughout. However, none are known to be very close to Earth. The nearest known black hole system is about 1,000 light-years away, which is quite distant on astronomical scales.

<hr>

The Loch Ness Monster, often called "Nessie," has sparked curiosity and debate for decades.

Scientifically, most theories consider Nessie a myth or misidentification of natural phenomena. Some speculate it could be large fish like sturgeon or catfish, or even logs and waves creating optical illusions. Others suggest it might be a surviving prehistoric creature like a plesiosaur, though this is highly unlikely due to the lack of evidence.

Despite extensive searches and sonar scans of Loch Ness, no conclusive proof of Nessie's existence has been found. The legend persists, blending folklore with the mystery of Scotland's deep waters.

Proving a negative is almost impossible, so regardless of how many sonar and mapping missions scientists attempt on Loch

Ness, they will never dissuade the people who think the world is a more interesting place because of mysteries like Nessie.

• ▬▬▬▬ • • ▬▬▬▬ •

The existence of Sasquatch, also known as Bigfoot, remains unproven by scientific standards. Reports of Sasquatch sightings and footprints have persisted for centuries across North America, leading to ongoing speculation and fascination. However, conclusive evidence such as bones, DNA, or clear photographs remains elusive.

Scientists generally regard Sasquatch as a cultural phenomenon or misidentification of known animals like bears or large apes. Despite extensive searches and occasional claims of evidence, the scientific community awaits verifiable proof before accepting Sasquatch as a real biological species.

• ▬▬▬▬ • • ▬▬▬▬ •

Bats eat a lot of insects. In fact, bats help farmers by reducing pesticide costs by up to $3.7 billion annually. These beneficial mammals are a critical part of the ecosystem, and are protected in some states. Currently, 85 bat species are endangered, and 113 bat species are considered vulnerable.

• ▬▬▬▬ • • ▬▬▬▬ •

An African elephant is the largest land animal on the planet. An average adult bull elephant weighs between 10,362 and 13,334 pounds. Also, elephants are matriarchal. That means the females are in charge of the herd. And never get in the way of a hungry elephant. While they are vegetarians, elephants can consume up to 300 pounds of leaves daily…an eating feat made easier by only sleeping 2 hours out of every 24.

61

Astrology is a belief system that suggests a connection between the positions and movements of celestial bodies (like stars and planets) and events on Earth, including human affairs and natural phenomena. It's based on the idea that the positions of these celestial bodies at the time of a person's birth can influence their personality, behavior, and destiny.

Astrology has ancient roots and is practiced in various forms worldwide. It contrasts with astronomy, which is the scientific study of celestial objects and phenomena without making claims about their influence on human life.

Here are the astrological zodiac signs corresponding to each month:

- Aries (March 21 - April 19)
- Taurus (April 20 - May 20)
- Gemini (May 21 - June 20)
- Cancer (June 21 - July 22)
- Leo (July 23 - August 22)
- Virgo (August 23 - September 22)
- Libra (September 23 - October 22)
- Scorpio (October 23 - November 21)
- Sagittarius (November 22 - December 21)
- Capricorn (December 22 - January 19)
- Aquarius (January 20 - February 18)
- Pisces (February 19 - March 20)

While people may deny astrology and its relevance in our lives, the character traits of people are often attributed to their "astrological sign." This phenomenon may be caused by self-fulfilling prophecy, where a person adapts his or her behavior to fit societal expectations.

The Earth's atmosphere is primarily composed of the following gases:

- Nitrogen (N2): Approximately 78% by volume
- Oxygen (O2): Approximately 21% by volume
- Argon (Ar): Approximately 0.93% by volume
- Carbon Dioxide (CO2): Approximately 0.04% by volume
- Trace Gases: Including neon, helium, methane, krypton, hydrogen, and xenon, among others, making up less than 0.01% collectively.

These percentages can vary slightly depending on factors such as location, altitude, and local conditions. Water vapor is also present in varying amounts, typically ranging from a fraction of a percent to several percent by volume, and plays a crucial role in weather and climate.

The Earth is composed of several distinct layers, each with different compositions and properties:

- Crust: This is the outermost layer, where we live. It varies in thickness from about 5 to 70 kilometers (3 to 43 miles) beneath the continents and about 5 to 10 kilometers (3 to 6 miles) beneath the oceans. The crust is primarily made of the continental crust, mainly granite and sedimentary rocks, and oceanic crust, made of basalt and gabbro.

- Mantle: Beneath the crust lies the mantle, extending down to about 2,900 kilometers (1,800 miles) below the surface. The mantle is mostly solid but can flow slowly over long periods. It consists mainly of silicate minerals rich in magnesium and iron.

- Outer Core: Below the mantle is the outer core, extending from about 2,900 to 5,150 kilometers (1,800 to 3,200 miles) deep. The outer core is liquid and composed mainly of iron and nickel.

- Inner Core: At the very center of the Earth lies the inner core, extending from about 5,150 to 6,371 kilometers (3,200 to 3,959 miles) deep. The inner core is solid and consists primarily of iron and nickel, similar to the outer core but under immense pressure, making it solid despite high temperatures.

These layers are differentiated based on their composition, temperature, and physical state, and they interact to create the Earth's geological processes and magnetic field.

In geometry and physics, the radius (plural: radii) refers to the distance from the center of a circle, sphere, or any round object to its outer edge or boundary. It is a fundamental measurement used to describe the size of these objects. For example:

- Circle: The radius is the distance from the center to any point on the circle's edge.
- Sphere: The radius is the distance from the center to any point on the sphere's surface.
- Cylinder: The radius refers to the distance from the center of the circular base to its edge.
- Any round object: The radius defines how far you would travel from the center to the outer edge in a straight line.

The radius is half of the diameter of a circle or sphere. It is a crucial parameter in calculations involving circumference, area, volume, and other geometric properties of round shapes.

The Earth has a radius of approximately 3,959 miles. Which means if you were trapped in the inner core of the planet, you would have to bore through almost four thousands miles of molten rock to reach the surface.

Traveling around the surface is the circumference of the planet. At the equator you would have ot travel 24,901 miles to return to the spot where you started.

Surface wise, the Earth has over 197 million square miles, making it the fifth largest planet in the Solar System, based on size. The radius of the Sun is 109 times that of Earth.

Have you ever wondered why the sky is blue?

The sky appears blue because of a phenomenon called Rayleigh scattering. Here's how it works:

- Sunlight Composition: Sunlight is made up of a spectrum of colors ranging from red to violet, which together appear as white light.
- Atmospheric Gases: Earth's atmosphere contains gases like nitrogen and oxygen, along with other particles.
- Scattering of Light: When sunlight enters Earth's atmosphere, shorter wavelengths of light (blue and violet) are scattered more efficiently by the small particles and gases in the atmosphere compared to longer wavelengths (like red and yellow).
- Dominance of Blue: As a result of this scattering, the blue and violet wavelengths are scattered in all directions by the atmosphere. This scattered blue light is what we

predominantly see when we look up at the sky during the day.

- Sky Color Variations: At sunrise and sunset, when the sun is lower on the horizon, sunlight passes through more of the atmosphere, scattering out more of the blue and leaving behind the longer wavelengths (red, orange, yellow), giving the sky its colorful hues.

In essence, the sky appears blue because of the scattering of sunlight by Earth's atmosphere, with shorter blue wavelengths being scattered more effectively than longer wavelengths, which makes the sky look blue to our eyes during the day.

***

The movie *A Beautiful Mind* with Russell Crowe and Jennifer Connelly, portrays the mathematician Dr. John Nash's equilibrium theory where rational players will make predictable decisions. Sadly, while his theories have been applied to both economics and international relations, the requirement that players must be rational, in my opinion, nullifies its value in a crazy, mixed up, world.

Game theory is a mathematical framework used to analyze strategic interactions among rational decision-makers. Central to game theory is the concept of the "game," which consists of players, strategies, and payoffs. Each player aims to maximize their payoff, considering the potential choices of others. One key idea is the Nash equilibrium, where no player benefits from changing their strategy unilaterally, leading to stable outcomes.

Beyond economics, game theory's applications span political science, biology, and computer science. In politics, it helps understand voting systems and coalition formations. In biology, it explains the evolution of cooperative behaviors among species. In computer science, it optimizes algorithms in network design and cybersecurity.

Game theory also tackles dilemmas like the Prisoner's Dilemma, where individual rationality leads to collective suboptimal outcomes, highlighting the tension between self-interest and collective welfare. Through these insights, game theory provides a profound lens for examining complex, interdependent systems.

Random Q & A

Question: What wild animal is virtually bullet proof?

Answer: Armadillos have a tough hide that can repel most smaller caliber bullets.

An armadillo is a small to medium-sized mammal known for its distinctive armored shell made of bony plates covered with tough, overlapping scales. They are native to the Americas, ranging from the southern United States to South America.

Armadillos are known for their ability to roll into a ball when threatened, using their armor as protection against predators. They have strong claws for digging and primarily feed on insects, small vertebrates, plants, and fruits. Armadillos are nocturnal or crepuscular (active at dawn and dusk) and are known for their unique appearance and behavior.

In Texas, many people believe the most authentic chili you can eat is made from armadillo meat.

Question: Did you know the second largest planet in our Solar System can float on water?

Answer: The planet Saturn is mostly comprised of gas and ice...which means despite being the second largest planet in our solar system, it could float on water.

Question: What galaxy is the Milky Way galaxy scheduled to hit?

Answer: In 3.75 billion years, the Milky Way galaxy will collide with the Andromeda galaxy.

Question: How fast does human hair grow?

Answer: Your hair will grow over 590 miles in your lifetime. That's a lot of hair, and suggests hair salons and barber shops will continue to do a booming business.

Question: What is the most common bird on the planet?

Answer: Contrary to popular belief, the most common wild bird on Earth is not a sparrow, it is the red billed quelea. The quelea is native to Africa, with an estimated population of 1.5 billion.

Question: What are the Man Eaters of Tsavo?

Answer: Lions once roamed every country on the continent of Africa, and even ventured into Europe and the Middle East. Today, lions are extinct in Europe and most of the Middle East, and are extinct in 26 African countries.

In the 1996 fictionalized movie version of a true story called *Ghost and the Darkness*, starring Val Kilmer and Michael Douglas, two maneless lions haunted railroad workers along the Tsavo, Kenya railway in 1898.

Historical records indicate the lions accounted for 135 deaths, but only 31 killings have been confirmed. Today, the lions are on display in the Chicago Field Museum.

Scientists believe the lions were driven to prey on humans because of bad teeth, that made it difficult for them to hunt and kill wild game. The availability of hundreds of human targets in the railway work camps offered a tantalizing feeding ground of relatively easy prey.

In 1991 a lion near Mfuwe, Zambia, ate 6 people before being killed. He is also on display at the Field Museum.

Question: What country contains more lakes than any other country?

Answer: Canada has over 879,000 lakes, and is home to 62% of the 1.42 million lakes globally.

Lake Superior is the largest lake in Canada, and is one of the five Great Lakes. An easy way to remember the names of the Great Lakes is the acronym: HOMES.

1. Huron
2. Ontario
3. Michigan
4. Erie
5. Superior

Question: On what date did astronauts Neil Armstrong and Buzz Aldrin first walk on the Moon?

Answer: Apollo 11 delivered Neil Armstrong and Buzz Aldrin to the surface of the Moon on 20 July 1969. Five other Apollo missions brought 10 other astronauts to the Moon. The twelve

astronauts who walked on the Moon include: Neil Armstrong, Buzz Aldrin, Charles "Pete" Conrad, Alan Bean, Alan Shepard, Edgar Mitchell, David Scott, James Irwin,
John Young, Charles Duke, Eugene Cernan, and Harrison Schmitt.

Question: What movie portrays a rash of global suicides due to chemicals being emitted by trees in an apparent war against humanity?

Answer: The Happening.

In 2008 M. Night Shyamalan released his dark portrayal of mass suicide in his movie, *The Happening*. As it turns out, nature in general, and trees in particular, have declared war against humans. Using a mass release of chemicals, nature deprives humans of their will to survive. It's a frightening and dark story.

Could this really happen?

In the African savannah, arcadia trees can measure how many of its leaves grazing animals are consuming. When it becomes excessive, the trees increase their tannin levels to discourage the foraging of its leaves. And as if that's not enough, the trees can release sprays of ethylene gas. The gas travels in the wind, warning other arcadia trees to increase their tannin levels in anticipation of increased leaf foraging.

Question: Why are owls so good about turning the eyes?

Answer: An owl can turn its head 270 degrees. Humans can manage 180 degrees, at best. Owls have evolved to do this because they cannot move their eyes.

Question: What is the collective noun for a group of crows?

Answer: A collective noun is the name given to a group of a unique species of animal. For example, a group of rats is known as a mischief, and a collection of apes is known as a troop. Crows earned the collective noun, murder, from a common medieval belief that crows were ill omens. They also have a murderous trait whereby a large collection of crows can band together and essentially hold a trial against another crow. If the murder of crows agree, they can descend upon the accused crow and kill him or her.

Question: Why do images of astronauts on the surface of the Moon show them jumping or bouncing?

Answer: Due to the density of the Moon, gravity on the Moon is 1/6 of gravity on Earth. An astronaut walking on the Moon would feel like he weighed 16% of his weight on Earth.

Neil Armstrong and Buzz Aldrin both discovered the quickest and easiest way to move around on the surface of the Moon in the bulky spacesuits was to jump. This of course terrified NASA engineers on the ground, as jumping dramatically increased the risk of falling and damaging the spacesuit. Falls turned out to be fairly commonplace, but fortunately, none resulted in harm to any astronaut or his suit.

Question: Welding is typically thought of a process where extreme heat is used to bond metals together. However, how is it possible to weld without the use of heat?

Answer: Cold welding is a process that enables two like metals to fuse using pressure, rather than heat.

Question: Why does the flower, commonly known as the corpse flower, stink to high heaven?

Answer: Don't bother sniffing the fragrance of a corpse flower. It uses the smell of death and rot to attract its prey.

Question: What animal has the ability to carry his comfort with him, in the form of a pillow?

Answer: Thanks to a very long and flexible neck, a giraffe can use its own butt as a pillow. Most adult giraffes sleep on the their feet, like horses. However, younger giraffe often lie down to sleep, and enjoy resting their heads on their own butts.

Question: What natural phenomenon kills more people than any other?

Answer: Natural disasters like tornadoes, flooding, and hurricanes can be frightening, but the real killer is heat. Between 70 to 80 people die each year in tornadoes or flooding, but on average, 130 people die from heat related injuries annually.

Question: Sharks may terrorize the seas, but what ground based critters deserve caution?

Answer: Sharks kill an average of 4 people per year, but cows kill an average of 22 people per year. Keep that in mind the next time you wander into a pasture.

Question: What is the name of the closest galaxy to the Milky Way?

Answer: Andromeda Galaxy. The Milky Way Galaxy is a spiral galaxy, with curved arms, like spokes on a wheel, arcing out from a center core. Our solar system rests on the outer edges of one of these bands. Our closest galactic neighbor is the Andromeda Galaxy at 2.5 million light years from Earth.

Question: What is the process by which plants make their own food called?

Answer: Photosynthesis.

Question: What is the study of fossils called?

Answer: Paleontology. While most people think of paleontologists as dinosaur hunters, in actuality, the field of studying fossils is much more involved than unearthing the next T. Rex skull.

The field of paleontology also includes:

1. Vertebrate paleontology focuses on early fish and mammals with backbones.
2. Invertebrate paleontology hunts down mollusk and arthropod fossils.
3. Paleobotany studies fossilized plants, algae, and fungi.
4. Palynology studies pollen and spores.
5. Micropaleontology deals with microscopic fossil organisms.

Question: What is the fastest animal on land?

Answer: Cheetah. When pursuing its prey, a cheetah can accelerate to over 60 miles per hour. At that speed, the cheetah is covering over 88 feet per second. If a cheetah participated in a 100 yard dash competition, she would cover the distance in approximately 3.4 seconds. The current human record for the 100 yard dash is 9 seconds.

Question: What is the phenomenon where the Moon appears to partially cover the Sun?

Answer: Solar eclipse.

Question: What is the scientific name for table salt?

Answer: NaCl (sodium chloride).

Question: A diamond is known as the hardest natural substance on the planet. But, what is a blood diamond?

Answer: A blood diamond is not red, as the name may suggest. It is any diamond mined in a war zone, typically using slave labor to finance an insurgency or a warlord's activity. Blood diamonds may also be called conflict diamonds, hot diamonds, or red diamonds. The term blood diamond has become widely recognized following a 2006 film by the same title, directed by Edward Zwick.

Question: What is the process by which rocks, minerals, and soil are broken down over time?

Answer: Weathering.

Question: What is the smallest planet in our solar system?

Answer: Mercury. This small planet orbits closer to the Sun than any other planet and is also known as the only planet in our solar system not to have a moon.

Question: What is the name of the phenomenon where the Earth's magnetic poles reverse?

Answer: Magnetic pole reversal.

Question: Where did the planets in our Solar System get their names?

Answer: The 8 planets in our solar system (9 if you still cling to Pluto's planetary status) are named for Greek and Roman gods and goddesses. Mars, named after the god of war, is also known as the Red Planet.

Question: Humans breathe oxygen. What gas is a common part of a human's exhalation?

Answer: Carbon dioxide is a gas humans and many other oxygen breathing animals exhale. Fortunately plants on Earth love carbon dioxide, and exhale oxygen. It's a beautiful system built on symbiosis, or mutualism.

Question: What is the largest living animal on the planet?

Answer: While the African elephant is the largest land animal on the planet, weighing over 13,000, the blue whale is the largest mammal, and animal all-around, on the planet. An adult blue whale can weigh over 199 tons, which is well over 200,000 pounds. Put in human terms, a blue whale is the weight of 1,388 high school football players, assuming an average weight of 216 pounds per player.

Question: Are dolphins and whales fish?

Answer: Dolphins and whales are NOT fish. In fact, they are air breathing mammals. A mammal is a vertebrate animal (meaning it has a backbone) that has warm blood, produces milk for its young, and gives live birth, as opposed to being hatched from an egg.

Question: What is the smallest bone in the human body?

Answer: The stapes is the smallest bone in the human body. The stapes is also known as the stirrup on account of its shape. It is part of the inner ear and is crucial to the conduction of sound vibrations. The stapes is approximately 3 millimeters in length, or a tenth of one inch.

Geography and World Facts

Geography is the study of Earth's landscapes, environments, and the relationships between people and their environments, and is crucial in understanding our world.

It integrates physical and human processes, guiding urban planning, environmental conservation, and disaster management. Geography helps us comprehend cultural diversity, economic systems, and global interconnections, fostering informed decision-making. By revealing spatial patterns and interactions, geography equips us to address pressing challenges like fresh water allocation and its use, population growth, resource distribution, natural disasters, and sustainable development.

The planet Earth is not round. In fact, is an oblate spheroid. Measured at the equator, the Earth is 7,926 miles in diameter. If you measured the diameter around the poles, you would get 7,900.

At the equator, the circumference of the Earth is 24,901 miles. The circumference around the poles 24,860 miles. The circumference of Earth around the poles is called the meridional circumference. Aristotle was the first person to attempt to measure the Earth's circumference. He placed it at 45,000 miles, or about double what it actually is. Another Greek thinker named Eratosthenes used geometry to measure the curvature of the Earth around 250 B.C. His measurement was 99% accurate. And just so you'll know, the study of Earth's size, gravity, and place in the solar system, is known as geodesy.

Earth is 80% iron, making it the densest planet in the solar system. Astronomers use the Earth's size to measure other planets and celestial bodies in terms of "how many Earths."

For example, Jupiter is 317.8 times the mass of Earth. Yet despite its size, its density is much lower than Earth's because it is a gaseous planet. Venus is .81 the mass of Earth.

Earth is the third rock from the Sun in our solar system. Including Pluto (which was recently demoted from planet status), there are 9 known planets in our solar system. In order:

1. Mercury
2. Venus
3. Earth
4. Mars
5. Jupiter
6. Saturn
7. Uranus
8. Neptune
9. Pluto

Astronomers at Caltech Univeristy believe there may be one or more unknown planets beyond Pluto. They base this theory on the orbital analysis of Kuiper Belt Objects (think asteroids) orbiting around the Sun beyond Neptune.

When it comes to mountains and highlands, the last place you may think of is Florida.

Florida has an average elevation above sea level of 100 feet. Its highest elevation is at a place called Britton Hill in North Florida. It is 345 feet above sea level.

As for the lowest place in America, you would have to travel west to Death Valley, California, Where an area known as Bad Water has an elevation of 282 feet below sea level. The lowest spot on the planet is located at the Dead Sea in Israel and Jordan. The Dead Sea is 414 meters, or 1,358 feet, below sea level.

In contrast, the highest point on the planet is Mt. Everest at 8,848 meters, or 29,031 feet. Within the contiguous United States (the lower 48), the highest point is Mt. Whitney at 14,505 feet above sea level…whose peak is visible from Bad Water in Death Valley.

Alaska's Mount Denali (formerly Mt. McKinley) reigns as the tallest mountain in America at 20,320 feet above sea level. Interestingly, Alaska contains 9 other peaks taller than Mt. Whitney.

The Earth tilts 23.5 degrees on its axis, and as the planet orbits the Sun, exposure to the Sun varies from season to season. In the winter, the northern hemisphere is pointed away from the Sun, so less sunlight causes cooler temperatures. While the northern hemisphere experiences cooler weather, the southern hemisphere is pointed at the Sun and experiences warmer temperatures.

There are two times of the year when the Earth's axis is tilted neither toward nor away from the Sun, causing both northern and southern hemispheres to receive an equal amount of sunlight. These times are known as the equinox, from the word equal, and are marked on our calendar as spring and fall.

The spring equinox occurs on March 20 or March 21 of each year. The fall equinox occurs on September 22 or 23.

In the northern hemisphere, the summer solstice occurs at the moment the Earth's tilt toward the Sun is at a maximum and occurs on June 20 or June 21 of each year. The winter solstice marks the shortest day and longest night of the year and occurs on December 21 or December 22 each year.

• ▬▬▬▬▬▬ • • ▬▬▬▬▬▬ •

The number 7 is used in many different contexts, and is essentially an archetype. According to psychologist Carl Jung, an archetype is a pattern of thought or symbolic imagery that becomes part of what Jung called our 'collective experience."

Some examples of the number seven in our world includes Isaac Newton's seven colors of the rainbow, the seven days of a week, the seven days of creation, the seven branches on a Menorah, the seven Chakras of meditation, the seven heavens in Islam, the seven wonders of the world, the seven continents on Earth, and the seven seas.

The seven seas of the planet are: North Atlantic Ocean, South Atlantic Ocean, North Pacific Ocean, South Pacific Ocean, Arctic Ocean, Southern Ocean, and the Indian Ocean. In ancient times, the seven seas were listed as: The Mediterranean Sea, The Adriatic Sea, The Black Sea, The Red Sea, The Arabian Sea, The Persian Gulf, and The Caspian Sea.

This list clearly reflects the focus on Europe and the Middle East as the known world, reflective of sailor's experiences at the time, as well as stories like *Sinbad the Sailor*.

If you manage to find yourself lost, try not to get lost near Point Nemo.

Point Nemo is a spot in the South Pacific considered the most remote spot on the planet, with its nearest neighbors in any direction over 1,000 miles away. It is also known as the graveyard for downed spacecraft, intentionally brought back to Earth over this spot to minimize the chance of space debris landing on people.

When the International Space Station is brought down around 2031, this is where it will fall. The word Nemo stands for "no one." The point is named in honor of the Jules Verne submarine captain from 20,000 Leagues Under The Sea. Point Nemo's nearest inhabited island is Pitcairn Island, home to the descendants of the Bounty mutineers, who chose the island to avoid interaction with other ships.

Semisopochnoi Island in the Alaska Aleutian Islands chain, is technically the easternmost spot in all of North America because it lies in the eastern hemisphere. This makes Alaska the western most, and eastern most, spot in America at the same time.

The Mauna Kea mountain in Hawaii is bigger than Mt. Everest. Mt. Everest stands at 29,031 feet above sea level. Mauna Kea is only 13,796 feet above sea level, but if you measure the mountain's height from the floor of the sea, it stands at 32,808 feet.

North and South America are slowing marching their way into the Pacific Ocean at 3 centimeters per year. That doesn't sound like much in terms of a lifetime, but in geological time, a few centimeters per year equates to planet altering changes.

The center of the contiguous United States was set in 1912 as Lebanon, Kansas. Since the addition of Alaska to the Union, the geographical center of the United States was moved north a bit in 1959 to a spot 20 miles north of Belle Fourche, South Dakota by the U.S. National Geodetic Survey…a federal agency.

The hottest temperature ever recorded on the planet is 134.1 degrees Fahrenheit on 10 July 1913 at Furnace Creek Ranch in Death Valley in the United States. Ironically, this is near the lowest spot in North America, Bad Water.

The coldest temperature ever recorded on the planet is −182 degrees Fahrenheit at the then-Soviet Vostok Station in Antarctica on 21 July 1983.

Absolute zero is a temperature of -459.67 degrees Fahrenheit.

The Fahrenheit scale used to measure temperature was created by a European physicist named Daniel Fahrenheit in 1724. Its two main fixed points are 32 degrees where water freezes, and 212 degrees where water boils.

The "Singing Sand Dunes" of New Mexico are a captivating geographical phenomenon where certain sand dunes produce a unique, resonant hum.

This sound, reminiscent of a deep, melodic drone, occurs when wind or human interaction causes the sand grains to vibrate and slide against each other. The specific conditions required — dry, well-rounded grains of a particular size and silica content — make this a rare occurrence. These dunes not only offer a stunning visual landscape but also an auditory experience that has fascinated both scientists and visitors alike.

Exploring these dunes reveals the intricate interplay between natural forces and geological formations, highlighting the wonders hidden within Earth's diverse terrains.

The moving rocks of Death Valley, known as the "sailing stones," have puzzled observers for decades. Found in Racetrack Playa, these rocks seemingly defy gravity, leaving long trails behind them as they glide across the desert floor.

For years, their movement was a mystery, with theories ranging from magnetic forces to alien intervention. However, recent studies have revealed that a unique combination of winter ice, wind, and sunlight is responsible. Thin sheets of ice form under the rocks during cold nights, and as temperatures rise, the ice breaks into floating panels that are propelled by light winds, gently pushing the rocks along the muddy surface.

This slow, almost imperceptible motion creates the illusion of these stones sailing autonomously, showcasing a fascinating interplay between climate and terrain in one of the hottest places on Earth.

Whatever the scientific explanation may be, there is something uncanny about heavy stones rolling across the desert floor.

———

Thomas Malthus, an 18th-century British economist, posited a theory on population growth that has sparked extensive debate and study. In his work "An Essay on the Principle of Population," Malthus argued that population growth tends to outpace food production, leading to inevitable shortages and societal strain. He believed that while population grows geometrically, food supply increases only arithmetically. This imbalance, he warned, would result in famine, disease, and other checks on population growth.

Malthus' theory, though critiqued for its pessimistic outlook and failure to anticipate technological advances in agriculture, laid foundational ideas for the study of demographics and economics. It underscored the importance of resource management and the potential consequences of unchecked growth.

Today, his ideas resonate in discussions on sustainability, environmental impact, and global food security, reminding us of the delicate balance between human populations and the Earth's resources.

———

Life expectancy statistics may be misleading.

Life expectancy statistics can be misleading, particularly when not accounting for disease prevalence and high infant mortality rates. These figures often represent averages that obscure the disparities within a population. For instance, in regions with high infant mortality, the average life expectancy may appear significantly lower, masking the fact that many individuals who survive infancy often live to an older age. This statistical phenomenon, known as the "infant mortality effect," can distort the true health profile of a society.

Additionally, the presence of chronic diseases or epidemics can skew life expectancy data. In areas where diseases like HIV/AIDS, malaria, or tuberculosis are prevalent, life expectancy can be dramatically reduced, reflecting the burden of these health challenges rather than the overall longevity potential of the population.

Moreover, improvements in healthcare, sanitation, and nutrition can rapidly increase life expectancy, making it a dynamic measure that may not accurately reflect long-term trends or the current health status of older adults. Thus, while life expectancy is a useful indicator, it requires careful interpretation alongside other metrics, such as disease incidence, healthcare access, and socioeconomic factors, to provide a comprehensive understanding of a population's health.

As of 2022, a male born in America today can expect to live 74.8 years. Females typically live to 80.2 years.

Males often have a shorter life expectancy than females due to a combination of biological, behavioral, and social factors. Higher rates of risky behaviors (hold my beer moments), such as motorcycle riding, smoking and alcohol consumption, alongside occupational hazards and a tendency to avoid medical care, contribute significantly. Biologically, males are more prone to heart disease and other health issues. Additionally, societal pressures and stress levels can impact men's overall health, leading to a lower average lifespan compared to women.

The highest temperatures ever recorded on Earth offer a glimpse into the planet's most extreme environments. The current record is held by Death Valley, California, where the temperature soared to 134°F (56.7°C) on July 10, 1913, at Furnace Creek Ranch.

This scorching heat is attributed to the region's unique topography, low elevation, and dry conditions, which trap and intensify the sun's rays. Other hot spots include Kuwait and Iran, where temperatures have approached similar extremes. These record-breaking heats are not just fascinating meteorological phenomena but also underscore the importance of studying and preparing for extreme weather conditions in the context of climate change.

Understanding these temperature extremes helps in developing strategies to mitigate heat-related impacts on human health, agriculture, and infrastructure.

Freshwater reserves are crucial for sustaining life, agriculture, and industry, yet they are unevenly distributed across the globe. The Great Lakes of North America—Superior, Michigan, Huron, Erie, and Ontario—are a significant source, containing about 20% of the world's surface fresh water. These vast lakes, formed by glacial activity, hold around 6 quadrillion gallons of water, providing vital resources for millions of people in the United States and Canada.

The Great Lakes' freshwater reserves are critical not only for local consumption but also for supporting diverse ecosystems, enabling transportation and trade, and offering recreational opportunities. However, these reserves face threats from pollution, invasive species, and climate change, which can alter water levels and quality.

Preserving the Great Lakes is essential for ensuring a stable freshwater supply. This involves international cooperation, stringent environmental protections, and sustainable management practices to balance human needs with ecological health. The stewardship of the Great Lakes serves as a model for managing other freshwater reserves worldwide, highlighting the importance of protecting these vital resources for future generations.

Antarctica, the coldest and driest continent, holds about 70% of the world's fresh water in its massive ice sheets. Spanning over 14 million square kilometers, it's larger than Europe and Australia combined. The ice, averaging 1.6 kilometers thick, plays a crucial role in regulating Earth's climate by reflecting sunlight back into space and maintaining global temperature balance.

Antarctica's ice sheets influence sea levels; if melted entirely, they could raise oceans by about 60 meters, impacting coastlines globally. Additionally, the continent's extreme cold stabilizes ocean currents, influencing weather patterns worldwide.

Monitoring Antarctica's ice dynamics is crucial for understanding climate change's impact. Accelerated melting could disrupt ocean currents, alter weather patterns, and lead to sea level rise, affecting millions worldwide. Preserving Antarctica's ice is vital for mitigating climate risks and maintaining global environmental stability.

A polar magnetic reversal, also known as geomagnetic reversal or magnetic flip, is a natural phenomenon where the Earth's magnetic field reverses its polarity. This means the magnetic north and south poles switch places, with the magnetic field weakening significantly during the process. These reversals have occurred sporadically throughout Earth's history, evidenced by magnetic minerals in rocks aligning in opposite directions in different geological layers.

During a reversal, the magnetic field may become unstable or weak, potentially exposing the Earth to higher levels of cosmic radiation. Despite this, reversals do not happen overnight but can take thousands of years to complete. The last full reversal occurred about 780,000 years ago, and the Earth is currently experiencing a gradual weakening of its magnetic field, which some scientists speculate could be a precursor to another reversal.

A Grand Solar Minimum is a period characterized by a prolonged decrease in solar activity, particularly in terms of sunspot numbers and solar irradiance. Sunspots are dark spots on the Sun's surface indicating regions of intense magnetic activity, which influence solar output and radiation levels reaching Earth.

During a Grand Solar Minimum, such as the Maunder Minimum (1645-1715) or Dalton Minimum (1790-1830), the number of sunspots observed decreases significantly compared to typical solar cycles. This reduction in solar activity can lead to cooler temperatures on Earth, as less solar radiation reaches our planet. Historically, Grand Solar Minima have been associated with colder periods in regional and global climates, potentially influencing weather patterns and agricultural productivity.

While the impact of a Grand Solar Minimum on global climate is a topic of ongoing research, it is important to note that the influence of solar variability on Earth's climate is just one factor among many, including greenhouse gas concentrations, volcanic activity, and ocean currents.

Random Q & A

Question: How many square feet are in one acre?

Answer: There are 43,560 square feet in one acre. To put that in perspective, an American football field contains 57,600 square feet, or about 1.3 acres. If you knock off the end zones at each end, you are looking at basically one acre. In real estate terms, a "section" of land is 640 acres. The standard homestead allotment was 160 acres, or one quarter of a section.

Disneyland in Southern California contains 500 acres, and Central Park in New York City contains 843 acres. The Wrangell St. Elias National Park in Alaska is the largest in the country, and contains 8,322,509 acres. 7 out of the top ten largest National Parks in America are located in Alaska.

Question: Has the size of homes in America grown over the years?

Answer: The average house in America in 1920 was 1,048 square feet. The average home size today is 2,657 square feet. In 1920 the average American household had 4.23 people. Today, that number has decreased to 2.58. Interestingly, while home sizes have more than doubled, family sizes have been almost cut in half.

Question: What is considered the rarest human blood type?

Answer: AB Negative is considered the rarest blood type. O Positive is the most common, and is considered the "universal donor" blood type.

Question: What are the three parts of the human outer ear?

Answer: The human outer ear is made up of cartilage and skin. Its three parts are the tragus, the helix, and the lobule. All three together are described as the pinna, or the auricle.

Question: Name the seven continents of the planet.

Answer: Asia, Africa, Europe, North America, South America, Antarctica, and Australia. Asia is the largest continent in both size and population. According to 2023 census data and estimates, the population of Asia is 4,753,079,726. It is 31,033,131 square kilometers in size.

To roughly convert kilometers into miles, multiply the kilometers by .6. For example, 31,033,131 times .6 equals 18,619,878 square miles.

Question: In what major U.S. city, outside of Alaska, do you have to travel south to enter Canada?

Answer: Detroit, Michigan.

Question: How many time zones are there in Russia?

Answer: From Big Diomede in the Bering Sea to the Ukraine border, there are 11 time zones in Russia.

Question: What city in Nevada is west of Los Angeles?

Answer: Nevada is nearly 300 miles from the Pacific Coast, but Los Angeles is actually 86 miles east of Reno.

Question: What is the longest river in the world?

Answer: The Nile River.

The Nile River, spanning approximately 4,135 miles, is the longest river in the world. Flowing northward through northeastern Africa, it traverses eleven countries, including Egypt and Sudan, before emptying into the Mediterranean Sea. The Nile is historically significant, supporting ancient civilizations and remains vital for agriculture and water supply today.

Question: Which country has the most natural lakes?

Answer: Canada.

Question: What is the smallest country in the world by land area?

Answer: Vatican City.

Question: Which continent is the driest?

Answer: Antarctica.

Question: What is the capital of Australia?

Answer: Canberra.

Question: In which country can you find the ancient city of Petra?

Answer: Jordan.

Question: Which country is known as the Land of the Rising Sun?

Answer: Japan.

Question: What is the highest mountain in North America?

Answer: Denali, previously known as Mount McKinley, stands at 20,310 feet.

Question: Which river flows through Paris?

Answer: The Seine River.

The Left Bank in Paris, or "La Rive Gauche," refers to the southern bank of the River Seine. Historically, it is known for its artistic, intellectual, and bohemian atmosphere. This area includes notable neighborhoods such as the Latin Quarter,

Montparnasse, and Saint-Germain-des-Prés, and has been home to many famous writers, artists, and philosophers.

Question: What is the largest desert in the world?

Answer: The Antarctic Desert.

Question: Which country has the largest population?

Answer: China.

Question: What is the official language of Brazil?

Answer: Portuguese.

Question: What is the capital city of Egypt?

Answer: Cairo.

Question: Which U.S. state has the longest coastline?

Answer: Alaska, with over 6,640 miles of coastline along the North Pacific, the Bering Sea, and the Arctic Ocean.

Question: In which country is the Taj Mahal located?

Answer: India.

Question: What is the currency of Japan?

Answer: Yen. Exchange rates vary, but there are approximately 160 Yen for each U.S. dollar.

Question: Which European country is divided into cantons?

Answer: Switzerland.

Question: What is the largest island in the Mediterranean Sea?

Answer: Sicily.

Question: Which African country was formerly known as Abyssinia?

Answer: Ethiopia.

Question: What is the capital of Canada?

Answer: Ottawa.

Question: Which river is the longest in South America?

Answer: The Amazon River.

Question: Which country has the most volcanoes?

Answer: Indonesia.

The most famous Indonesian volcano is Krakatoa.

Krakatoa, also known as Krakatau, is a volcanic island situated in the Sunda Strait between the islands of Java and Sumatra in Indonesia. This volcanic system is part of the Pacific Ring of Fire, a region notorious for its seismic activity, which includes frequent earthquakes and numerous active volcanoes.

Krakatoa's most famous eruption occurred in August 1883 and is one of the most catastrophic volcanic events in recorded history. The eruption began on August 26th and reached its climax the following day, August 27th. The explosion was so powerful that it was heard as far away as Australia and the island of Rodrigues near Mauritius, over 3,000 miles away.

Question: What is the deepest lake in the world?

Answer: Lake Baikal.

Lake Baikal, often referred to as the "Pearl of Siberia," is a marvel of nature nestled in the mountainous region of Siberia, Russia. Located in the southern part of the Russian region of Siberia, near the city of Irkutsk, Lake Baikal is situated between the Irkutsk Oblast to the northwest and the Republic of Buryatia to the southeast. It is positioned in a rift valley, created by the Baikal Rift Zone, which is one of the most active seismic areas on the planet.

One of the most striking features of Lake Baikal is its depth. It holds the title of the deepest freshwater lake in the world, with a maximum depth of 1,642 meters (5,387 feet). This profound depth contributes to the lake's status as the largest freshwater lake by volume, containing approximately 20% of the world's unfrozen surface freshwater. The sheer volume of water in Lake Baikal is staggering, with more than 23,600 cubic kilometers of water.

Question: Which city is known as the Eternal City?

Answer: Rome.

Question: What is the name of the mountain range that separates Europe and Asia?

Answer: The Ural Mountains.

Question: What is the capital of Iceland?

Answer: Reykjavik.

Question: Which country is famous for tulips and windmills?

Answer: The Netherlands.

Question: What is the smallest ocean in the world?

Answer: The Arctic Ocean.

Question: Which city is known as the City of Love?

Answer: Paris.

Question: Which river forms the boundary between Texas and Mexico?

Answer: The Rio Grande.

The Rio Grande River, stretching about 1,896 miles, forms a natural border between the United States and Mexico. Originating in the Colorado Rockies, it flows through New Mexico and Texas, reaching the Gulf of Mexico. Vital for irrigation and water supply, the river also holds significant cultural and historical importance.

Literature and Authors

While Mark Twain was always quick to condemn a classic as a book that everybody praised, but nobody read, his cynicism missed the mark with his classic American novel, *Adventures of Huckleberry Finn.*

According to author Mark Twain, his inspiration for the Huckleberry Finn character was a childhood friend named Tom Blankenship.

Tom had the misfortune of being born into poverty, at the hands of alcoholic and dysfunctional parents. A Mark Twain scholar named George Hendrick once described the Huckleberry character as "underfed, unwashed, unschooled, unchurched, and a master at swearing." Mark Twain would agree.

Twain published *Adventures of Huckleberry Finn* in 1884, but the fictional character made his debut in *The Adventures of Tom Sawyer*, published in 1876.

Notable actors who have portrayed Huckleberry Finn in TV and film include: Mickey Rooney, Ron Howard, and Elijah Wood, among 20 others.

In the nine circles of Hell identified by Dante Alighieri in his 14th century poem *Inferno*, Hell is divided into circles, or levels, where the souls of eternally damned people are imprisoned according to the evil they condoned and perpetrated while on Earth.

Dante named these circles: Limbo, Lust, Gluttony, Greed, Anger, Heresy, Violence, Fraud, and Treachery. According to Dante, a person who died without knowing the Gospel of Christ would reside in Limbo. A murderer would find himself in the Treachery circle, closest to Satan.

Among the most popular and bestselling books of all time, the Holy Bible tops the list with an estimated 5 billion copies sold, shared, or distributed around the world.

The first novel on the list of top sellers is *The Tale of Two Cities*, by Charles Dickens. Around the world, 210 million copies of this story have been sold.

I discovered the bookstore as an early teen, and happily handed over every penny I had earned doing chores and returning soda pop bottles for refunds to fund my mad shopping sprees.

My favorite browsing spot in the bookstore was a rack of books near the front called, The Bantam Classics. Apparently, a company named Bantam (a registered trademark name) selected the best literary works and republished them in small, affordable paperbacks.

I was hooked. Here are a just a few titles that grabbed my attention.

The Adventures of Huckleberry Finn by Mark Twain
The Adventures of Sherlock Holmes by Arthur Conan Doyle
Black Beauty by Anna Sewell
Brave New World by Aldous Huxley
The Call of the Wild by Jack London
Candide by Voltaire
David Copperfield by Charles Dickens
Dracula by Bram Stoker
Frankenstein by Mary Shelley
The Grapes of Wrath by John Steinbeck
Great Expectations by Charles Dickens
Gulliver's Travels by Jonathan Swift
Moby-Dick by Herman Melville
The Odyssey by Homer
Oliver Twist by Charles Dickens
The Prince by Niccolò Machiavelli
The Scarlet Letter by Nathaniel Hawthorne
The Strange Case of Dr Jekyll and Mr Hyde by Robert Louis Stevenson
The Three Musketeers by Alexandre Dumas
Treasure Island by Robert Louis Stevenson

In the summer of 1816, Mary Shelley, then Mary Wollstonecraft Godwin, found herself in the company of literary giants. She and her future husband, Percy Bysshe Shelley, were staying at the Villa Diodati near Lake Geneva with Lord Byron and his physician, Dr. John Polidori. The weather was unseasonably cold and stormy, leading the group to spend much of their time indoors. To pass the time, Byron proposed a ghost story contest, challenging each person to write their own supernatural tale.

Mary struggled to come up with an idea, feeling the pressure of the company she was in. One night, after a particularly intense discussion about the principles of life, she had a vivid waking dream. In her vision, she saw a pale student of unhallowed arts kneeling beside the thing he had put together—a hideous phantasm of a man. This nightmare inspired her to write what would become "Frankenstein; or, The Modern Prometheus."

Despite initial hesitation and the encouragement of her companions, Mary persisted. Her story not only won the informal contest but also went on to become one of the most enduring classics of Gothic literature. The young woman who once doubted her ability to craft a ghost story created a narrative that has haunted and fascinated readers for generations.

<hr>

Two of the greatest writers in English literature, J.R.R. Tolkien and C.S. Lewis were best of friends and spent a lot of time hunched over a small table in a pub, discussing literature and the art of wrting. Wow. As a fan of both their works, it amazes me that these two power houses hung out together.

On a more serious note…

C.S. Lewis, the renowned author of "The Chronicles of Narnia," was known for his intellectual rigor and deep faith, but his path to writing these beloved children's books was anything but straightforward. One winter evening in 1939, during a casual walk with his close friend and fellow writer, J.R.R. Tolkien, through the frosty paths of Oxford, Lewis confessed a strange dream he had been having repeatedly.

In his dream, he saw a fawn carrying an umbrella and parcels in a snowy wood. Tolkien, intrigued, encouraged Lewis to explore this peculiar vision further. Lewis, who was at the time immersed in scholarly work and writing theological texts, was hesitant. However, Tolkien's enthusiasm was infectious, and Lewis began to jot down notes about this curious character and the world he might inhabit.

Over the next few years, the simple image from his dream expanded into a rich, fantastical world filled with talking animals, brave children, and epic battles between good and evil. Lewis's academic peers were surprised when he first shared his foray into children's literature, but his genuine passion for storytelling shone through.

The result was "The Lion, the Witch, and the Wardrobe," the first of seven books in "The Chronicles of Narnia" series. These books, inspired by a dream and nurtured by the encouragement of a friend, have since captivated the imaginations of millions, becoming a testament to the power of dreams and the importance of friendship in creative endeavors.

J.R.R. Tolkien's inspiration for writing "The Hobbit" and "The Lord of the Rings" came from a curious mix of academic pursuits, personal experiences, and a single serendipitous moment. One evening in the early 1930s, Tolkien, a professor of Anglo-Saxon at Oxford University, was grading a seemingly endless stack of student essays. As the hours dragged on, his mind began to wander, and he found himself doodling on a blank page.

In the midst of this academic tedium, he scribbled a simple sentence: "In a hole in the ground there lived a hobbit." This unexpected phrase piqued his curiosity. What was a hobbit? Why did it live in a hole? Intrigued, Tolkien began to weave a story around this small, unassuming creature. Drawing upon his extensive knowledge of mythology, languages, and his own experiences during World War I, he crafted the tale of Bilbo Baggins and his unexpected journey.

As Tolkien shared "The Hobbit" with his children, their enthusiasm spurred him to develop the world of Middle-earth further. His love for languages and mythological storytelling deepened the narrative, giving birth to a richly detailed world filled with elves, dwarves, and ancient lore.

Years later, encouraged by the success of "The Hobbit" and urged by his publisher, Tolkien embarked on a much more ambitious project: "The Lord of the Rings." The story began as a sequel but evolved into an epic saga. His experiences during the war, especially the camaraderie and the profound sense of loss, heavily influenced the themes of friendship, sacrifice, and the struggle against overwhelming darkness.

Tolkien's meticulous world-building and creation of languages gave Middle-earth a depth and authenticity that captivated readers. What started as a simple doodle during a mundane task grew into one of the most influential and beloved works of fantasy literature, proving that inspiration can strike at the most unexpected times and lead to the creation of enduring masterpieces.

In 1990, J.K. Rowling was on a delayed train from Manchester to London when a young, bespectacled boy wizard simply "strolled into her mind."

She envisioned a magical school, characters, and a world hidden within our own. Without a pen to capture her thoughts, she spent the journey mentally piecing together Harry Potter's story. Over the next five years, through personal struggles and job changes, Rowling nurtured her idea, often scribbling notes on napkins and scraps of paper.

Her vivid imagination and perseverance, fueled by this fateful train ride, eventually led to the creation of the beloved Harry Potter series, captivating millions worldwide and transforming Rowling's life.

Arthur Conan Doyle, born in 1859 in Edinburgh, Scotland, was a physician before he became one of the most famous writers in the world. While studying medicine at the University of Edinburgh, Doyle encountered Dr. Joseph Bell, a master of observation and deduction. Bell's remarkable diagnostic abilities left a profound impression on Doyle, planting the seeds for his most famous character.

In 1887, Doyle introduced Sherlock Holmes in "A Study in Scarlet," drawing heavily from Bell's keen eye for detail and logical reasoning. Holmes, with his sharp intellect and methodical approach to solving mysteries, captivated readers. Despite initially seeing Holmes as a distraction from his more serious literary ambitions, Doyle's detective stories gained immense popularity.

Doyle's Holmes stories, set against the backdrop of Victorian London, combined intricate plots with a deep understanding of human nature. Through Holmes, Doyle explored themes of justice, logic, and the complexities of the human mind. While he wrote many other works, including historical novels and science fiction, it was Sherlock Holmes who secured Doyle's legacy, turning a physician's admiration for his mentor into a literary phenomenon that continues to intrigue readers to this day.

A book earns the title of "classic" through a combination of enduring qualities and cultural significance. These key factors contribute to a book's classic status:

- Timeless Themes: Classics address universal themes such as love, justice, morality, and the human condition. These themes resonate with readers across different eras and cultures, allowing the book to remain relevant long after its publication.

- Literary Merit: A classic book typically showcases exceptional writing. This includes masterful use of language, innovative narrative techniques, and well-crafted characters. The author's skill in storytelling and the book's artistic qualities contribute to its lasting appeal.

- Cultural Impact: Classics often influence culture and society, shaping literary trends, inspiring other works, and contributing to public discourse. They leave a lasting imprint on the arts and humanities, reflecting and sometimes challenging societal norms.

- Endurance: A book must withstand the test of time to be considered a classic. It continues to be read, studied, and appreciated by successive generations. Its relevance and popularity do not diminish over the years.

- Critical Acclaim: Classics are often recognized and praised by critics, scholars, and literary institutions. They receive accolades and are included in academic curricula, further cementing their status.

- Universal Appeal: Classics often transcend their original context, appealing to a broad audience regardless of age, background, or geography. Their ability to speak to a wide range of readers helps secure their place in the literary canon.

Through a blend of these attributes, a book achieves the revered status of a classic, maintaining its influence and significance across time and space.

Have you ever heard the expression, "The only thing necessary for the triumph of evil is for good men to do nothing?"

Despite the popular belief that a Founding Father, like Thomas Jefferson or John Adams, said this, in fact, the quote is attributed to Edmund Burke.

Edmund Burke was a statesman and philosopher during the 1700s. He was born in Dublin, Ireland, and served as a member of parliament between 1766 and 1794. Interestingly, Burke opposed heavy taxation of the American colonies and supported the colonist's right to self government.

F. Scott Fitzgerald, born in 1896 in St. Paul, Minnesota, emerged as one of the defining voices of the Jazz Age. Growing up in a modest family, he attended Princeton University, where his literary ambitions began to take shape. His early success came with the publication of "This Side of Paradise" in 1920, which brought him fame and fortune. However, it was his keen observations of the excesses and decadence of the Roaring Twenties that fueled his magnum opus, "The Great Gatsby."

Fitzgerald's own life mirrored the extravagance and turmoil of his characters. His marriage to Zelda Sayre, a vibrant and often troubled socialite, exposed him to the opulent lifestyles and moral ambiguities that he depicted in his novel. The opulent parties he attended and the people he encountered in New York City provided rich material for his exploration of the American Dream's corruption. Through Jay Gatsby's tragic pursuit of love and success, Fitzgerald captured the disillusionment of an era, cementing his legacy as a master chronicler of American society.

Random Q & A

Question: Who wrote "To Kill a Mockingbird"?

Answer: Harper Lee.

Question: What is the title of the first novel by Jane Austen?

Answer: "Sense and Sensibility."

Question: Which Russian author wrote "War and Peace"?

Answer: Leo Tolstoy.

Question: Who is the author of the "Harry Potter" series?

Answer: J.K. Rowling.

Question: What is the name of the fictional town in "To Kill a Mockingbird"?

Answer: Maycomb.

Question: Which book begins with the line, "Call me Ishmael"?

Answer: "Moby-Dick."

Question: Who wrote "1984"?

Answer: George Orwell.

Question: What is the name of the rabbit in "Alice's Adventures in Wonderland"?

Answer: The White Rabbit.

Question: Who is the author of "The Great Gatsby"?

Answer: F. Scott Fitzgerald.

Question: In which book would you find the character Atticus Finch?

Answer: "To Kill a Mockingbird."

Question: Who wrote "Pride and Prejudice"?

Answer: Jane Austen.

Question: What is the setting of "The Catcher in the Rye"?

Answer: New York City.

Question: Who is the author of "Brave New World"?

Answer: Aldous Huxley.

Question: Which novel features the character Jay Gatsby?

Answer: "The Great Gatsby."

Question: Who wrote "The Picture of Dorian Gray"?

Answer: Oscar Wilde.

Question: What is the title of the first book in the "Chronicles of Narnia" series?

Answer: "The Lion, the Witch and the Wardrobe."

Question: Who is the author of "The Hobbit"?

Answer: J.R.R. Tolkien.

Question: Which novel features the character Elizabeth Bennet?

Answer: "Pride and Prejudice."

Question: Who wrote "The Adventures of Huckleberry Finn"?

Answer: Mark Twain.

Question: What is the title of the dystopian novel written by George Orwell about a totalitarian regime?

Answer: "1984."

Question: Who is the author of "Jane Eyre"?

Answer: Charlotte Brontë.

Question: Which novel features the character Holden Caulfield?

Answer: "The Catcher in the Rye."

Question: Who wrote "Crime and Punishment"?

Answer: Fyodor Dostoevsky.

Question: What is the title of the first book in the "Harry Potter" series?

Answer: "Harry Potter and the Philosopher's Stone."

Question: Who is the author of "The Odyssey"?

Answer: Homer.

Question: In which book would you find the character Frodo Baggins?

Answer: "The Lord of the Rings."

Question: Who wrote "Moby-Dick"?

Answer: Herman Melville.

Question: What is the name of the main character in "The Catcher in the Rye"?

Answer: Holden Caulfield.

Question: Who is the author of "Wuthering Heights"?

Answer: Emily Brontë.

Question: Which novel features the character Sherlock Holmes?

Answer: "A Study in Scarlet" (among others).

Question: Who wrote "Anna Karenina"?

Answer: Leo Tolstoy.

Question: What is the name of the island in "Lord of the Flies"?

Answer: The island is unnamed in the novel.

Question: Who is the author of "The Grapes of Wrath"?

Answer: John Steinbeck.

Question: Which novel features the character Tom Joad?

Answer: "The Grapes of Wrath."

Question: Who wrote "The Call of the Wild"?

Answer: Jack London.

Question: What is the title of the book that features the character Scout Finch?

Answer: "To Kill a Mockingbird."

Question: Who is the author of "Fahrenheit 451"?

Answer: Ray Bradbury.

Question: Which novel features the character Dr. Jekyll?

Answer: "The Strange Case of Dr Jekyll and Mr Hyde."

Question: Who wrote "Don Quixote"?

Answer: Miguel de Cervantes.

Question: What is the setting of "The Catch-22"?

Answer: World War II.

Question: Who is the author of "Slaughterhouse-Five"?

Answer: Kurt Vonnegut.

Question: Which novel features the character Hester Prynne?

Answer: "The Scarlet Letter."

Question: Who wrote "The Brothers Karamazov"?

Answer: Fyodor Dostoevsky.

Question: What is the title of the book that features the character Pip?

Answer: "Great Expectations."

Question: Who is the author of "The Sun Also Rises"?

Answer: Ernest Hemingway.

Question: Which novel features the character Captain Ahab?

Answer: "Moby-Dick."

Question: Who wrote "One Hundred Years of Solitude"?

Answer: Gabriel García Márquez.

Question: What is the title of the dystopian novel written by Aldous Huxley?

Answer: "Brave New World."

Question: Who is the author of "Gone with the Wind"?

Answer: Margaret Mitchell.

Question: Which novel features the character Ishmael?

Answer: "Moby-Dick."

Question: Who wrote "The Old Man and the Sea"?

Answer: Ernest Hemingway.

Question: What is the name of the magical school in the "Harry Potter" series?

Answer: Hogwarts School of Witchcraft and Wizardry.

Question: Who is the author of "Dracula"?

Answer: Bram Stoker.

Question: Which novel features the character Holden Caulfield?

Answer: "The Catcher in the Rye."

Question: Who wrote "The Picture of Dorian Gray"?

Answer: Oscar Wilde.

Question: What is the title of the first book in the "Lord of the Rings" series?

Answer: "The Fellowship of the Ring."

Question: Who is the author of "Moby-Dick"?

Answer: Herman Melville.

Question: Which novel features the character Elizabeth Bennet?

Answer: "Pride and Prejudice."

Question: Who wrote "Brave New World"?

Answer: Aldous Huxley.

Question: What is the setting of "The Great Gatsby"?

Answer: Long Island and New York City during the 1920s.

Sports and Athletes

Sports fans love a championship game, especially when the game features star players like Travis Kelce, and celebrities like Taylor Swift.

On 11 February 2024 the AFC champions Kansas City Chiefs met the NFC champions San Francisco 49ers at Allegiant Stadium in Las Vegas for football supremacy.

Allegiant Stadium in Las Vegas seats 65,000. Premium seating for the game went for $180,000 and up, while suite prices ranged from $1.8 to $3 million each. One can only hope the suite price came with free bottled water and pizza.

But there was more to the game than the stadium. Over the festive weekend, 300,000 people descended on Las Vegas, and over 500 private jets packed the tarmac of Harry Reid International Airport. Sadly, the day before the game a Nigerian banker, Herbert Wigwe, and five other passengers and crew died in a helicopter crash in the desert between Los Angeles and Las Vegas while enroute to the game.

Altogether, visitors and game enthusiasts dropped over $600 million in hotel and gambling expenses. CBS broadcast the game, with an estimated 200 million viewers worldwide, while the popular 30 second commercials cost advertisers up to $7 million each.

The game winner: Kansas City won the game in overtime 25 to 22.

In 1867, on Scotland's remote Isle of Islay, a farmer named Angus MacLeod stumbled upon an ancient oak chest buried in his fields. Inside, he found a collection of meticulously crafted wooden clubs and balls. Intrigued, Angus began experimenting with these relics, unknowingly rediscovering an early form of golf. As he played, he noticed his sheep began to follow him, intrigued by the bouncing balls.

Word of Angus's discovery spread, and soon neighbors joined him, leading to the formation of what would become one of Scotland's oldest golf clubs, the Machrie Golf Links. The course, nestled among rugged landscapes, still exists today, celebrating the serendipitous moment a farmer's curiosity revitalized a forgotten pastime and captivated an island community.

In 1978, during the US Open at Flushing Meadows, rising star John McEnroe faced an unexpected opponent: a mischievous pigeon. Mid-match, the bird swooped down onto the court, narrowly missing McEnroe's head. The umpire paused the game, and amidst the laughter, McEnroe famously quipped, "Even the birds want to see me play!"

The incident lightened the tension, and McEnroe went on to win the match with a blend of skill and newfound humor. This quirky event highlighted the unpredictable nature of tennis and endeared McEnroe to fans, showcasing his ability to turn a potential distraction into a memorable moment.

Today, the story of the pigeon at Flushing Meadows remains a beloved anecdote, illustrating the sport's capacity for both intense competition and unexpected levity…which is always better than McEnroe's notorious on-court displays of his temper and sense of justice.

In the 1950 World Cup, held in Brazil, the semi-final match between Uruguay and Sweden witnessed an extraordinary display of sportsmanship. During a tense moment, Swedish forward Hasse Jeppson accidentally collided with Uruguayan goalkeeper Roque Máspoli, causing a severe cramp. As the referee paused the game, Uruguayan captain Obdulio Varela, renowned for his fierce competitiveness, walked over to Jeppson, helping him stretch out his cramp.

This unexpected act of kindness was met with applause from both sets of fans. Inspired by their captain's gesture, Uruguay went on to win the match 3-2, securing their place in the final. They eventually triumphed over Brazil in the famous "Maracanazo" upset. Varela's sportsmanship in that semi-final remains a legendary moment, underscoring the spirit of fair play that the World Cup embodies.

In the 1992 NBA Finals, Michael Jordan of the Chicago Bulls showcased a performance that would be etched in basketball history. During Game 1 against the Portland Trail Blazers, Jordan exploded for 35 points in the first half, including an astonishing six three-pointers. After sinking his sixth, Jordan turned to the broadcast table and shrugged, a gesture that became iconic.

What many don't know is that this moment was inspired by a pre-game chat with his mother, who had told him, "Just have fun out there." Jordan's unprecedented scoring spree was a combination of skill and an embrace of his mother's advice. The Bulls won the game 122-89 and eventually the series, claiming their second consecutive championship.

The "shrug game" remains a testament to Jordan's greatness and his ability to turn maternal wisdom into basketball brilliance.

In 1920, a car dealership in Canton, Ohio, became the birthplace of the NFL. Ralph Hay, owner of the dealership and the Canton Bulldogs, invited representatives from various football teams to his showroom to discuss forming a league.

During the meeting, the men realized they didn't have enough chairs and ended up sitting on car fenders and running boards. Jim Thorpe, a legendary athlete and then a player-coach for the Bulldogs, was elected the first president of the new league, originally called the American Professional Football Association. The gathering was informal, but it laid the groundwork for the National Football League.

The historic meeting in a car showroom symbolizes the humble beginnings of what would become one of the most influential sports leagues in the world. Today, the NFL honors its roots with the Pro Football Hall of Fame located in Canton, commemorating the small-town meeting that started it all.

In the early 1920s, on the sunny beaches of Santa Monica, California, a group of lifeguards seeking a fun way to stay fit after their shifts pioneered beach volleyball.

Led by Paul "Pablo" Johnson, they set up a net between two lifeguard towers and started playing what would become a new sport. Using techniques from indoor volleyball, they adapted the game to the sandy environment, creating unique strategies and moves. Their casual games drew crowds, turning beach volleyball into a popular spectacle. By 1947, the first official beach volleyball tournament was held at State Beach, with organized rules and regulations.

The sport's popularity soared, spreading to beaches worldwide. The early lifeguards' innovative pastime evolved into a professional sport, making beach volleyball a beloved and integral part of coastal culture and an Olympic event by 1996.

In the mid-16th century, on the sheep-grazed commons of Guildford, England, local shepherds devised a game to pass the time. Using their crooks as bats and a wooden stool as a wicket, they aimed to strike a ball of wool bound with string.

This rudimentary pastime, known as "creckett," quickly gained popularity among villagers. By 1598, the game had formalized, with a written reference to "creckett" appearing in a legal dispute.

The game evolved with standardized rules and equipment, including the introduction of the first known cricket club in Hambledon in the 1760s. The sport's appeal grew, reaching London, where matches drew significant crowds. By the 18th century, cricket had become England's national sport, with international matches following soon after. The humble shepherds' innovation blossomed into a global sport, uniting millions with its rich tradition and competitive spirit.

In 1839, in Cooperstown, New York, a young farm boy named Abner Doubleday improvised a game to entertain his friends. Inspired by British rounders and local bat-and-ball games, he formalized rules and introduced four bases in a diamond shape.

This game, which he called "base ball," quickly captivated the local community. By the 1840s, Alexander Cartwright, a New York City firefighter and member of the Knickerbocker Base Ball Club, further refined the rules, establishing key elements like foul lines and the three-strike rule.

On June 19, 1846, the Knickerbockers played the first recorded baseball game against the New York Nine in Hoboken, New Jersey. The sport's popularity surged, leading to the formation of the National Association of Base Ball Players in 1857. From its modest beginnings in Cooperstown, baseball evolved into America's national pastime, celebrated for its rich history and cultural significance.

In the 1988 World Series, Game 1 between the Los Angeles Dodgers and the Oakland Athletics became the stage for an unforgettable moment. Dodger's star Kirk Gibson, suffering from severe injuries to both legs, was not expected to play. However, with the Dodgers trailing 4-3 in the bottom of the ninth and a runner on base, Gibson convinced manager Tommy Lasorda to let him pinch-hit. Limping to the plate against the dominant closer Dennis Eckersley, Gibson worked the count to 3-2. On the next pitch, he launched a dramatic two-run homer into the right-field stands. As he hobbled around the bases,

Gibson pumped his fist in pure elation, creating an iconic sports image.

This improbable walk-off home run not only won the game for the Dodgers but also set the tone for the series. The Dodgers went on to win the championship, and Gibson's heroic moment remains one of baseball's most legendary feats.

In 1926, during a game against the Washington Senators, Babe Ruth showcased his legendary charisma and power in an unexpected way. Ruth promised a sick child, Johnny Sylvester, he would hit a home run for him.

During the game, Ruth not only hit one but three home runs. What made this moment even more remarkable was Ruth's theatrical flair; before his third home run, he pointed to the center-field bleachers, "calling his shot." The crowd roared as Ruth delivered on his promise.

News of Ruth's heroics quickly reached Johnny, who credited the Babe's gesture with helping him recover. This event not only solidified Ruth's status as a baseball legend but also highlighted his compassionate nature. The story of Ruth's promise to Johnny Sylvester remains a poignant example of the impact sports heroes can have beyond the field.

Random Q & A

Question: When and where did the first college level football game occur?

Answer: The first college football game was played on 6 November 1869, in New Brunswick, New Jersey. The game was between Rutgers and Princeton. Rutgers won the game, 6-4. An odd football score that suggests two safeties and one touchdown, with no point after score. Oddly, the football was not the shape we know today, and resembled a modern day soccer ball. There were approximately 100 onlookers for the game.

Question: What professional football player holds the record for most pass receptions in post season play?

Answer: For years wide receiver and Hall of Fame inductee Jerry Rice held the record for most pass receptions in NFL playoff games at 151. On 28 January 2024, Kansas City Chief tight end Travis Kelce surpassed this record during the AFC Championship game against the Baltimore Ravens.

During the same game, the Baltimore quarterback Lamar Jackson caught his own pass. The pass was blocked and careened into the air, allowing Jackson time to get under it and turn a broken play into a gain of ten yards.

Question: What is the scientific name for the shape of a football?

Answer: The modern day football is an elongated spheroid, or prolate spheroid.

Question: Who holds the record for the most Grand Slam singles titles in tennis?

Answer: Margaret Court, with 24 titles.

Question: In which year did Michael Phelps set the record for the most Olympic gold medals won by an individual in a single Olympics?

Answer: 2008 (Beijing Olympics), with 8 gold medals.

Question: Who holds the record for the fastest century in Test cricket?

Answer: Brendon McCullum, who scored a century in 54 balls against Australia in 2016.

Question: What is the longest winning streak in NBA history, and which team achieved it?

Answer: The Los Angeles Lakers hold the record with a 33-game winning streak during the 1971-72 season.

Question: Who holds the record for the most career goals scored in men's international football (soccer)?

Answer: Ali Daei from Iran, with 109 goals.

Question: Which athlete has won the most Olympic medals in history?

Answer: Michael Phelps, with a total of 28 Olympic medals.

Question: What is the fastest recorded serve in tennis, and who hit it?

Answer: The fastest recorded serve was 163.7 mph (263.4 km/h) by Sam Groth of Australia in 2012.

Question: Who holds the record for the most points scored in a single NBA game?

Answer: Wilt Chamberlain, who scored 100 points for the Philadelphia Warriors against the New York Knicks in 1962. Notably, this was long before the NBA started its three point score system.

Question: What is the record for the most consecutive wins in a single NFL season?

Answer: The 2007 New England Patriots won 16 consecutive games in the regular season.

Question: Who holds the record for the most runs scored in a single MLB season?

Answer: Barry Bonds, who scored 73 home runs in the 2001 season.

Question: Which golfer has won the most Masters Tournaments?

Answer: Jack Nicklaus, with six victories.

Question: Who holds the record for the most points scored in a single NHL season?

Answer: Wayne Gretzky, who scored 215 points in the 1985-1986 season.

Question: What is the highest score achieved in a single game of bowling?

Answer: The highest score achieved in sanctioned competition is 300, also known as a perfect game.

Question: Who holds the record for the most consecutive Grand Slam titles won in tennis?

Answer: Rod Laver won all four Grand Slam titles in 1969.

Question: What is the record for the fastest knockout in UFC history?

Answer: Jorge Masvidal holds the record with a 5-second knockout of Ben Askren in 2019.

Question: Who holds the record for the most goals scored in a single NHL game?

Answer: Joe Malone and Wayne Gretzky share the record, both scoring 7 goals in a single game.

Question: Which athlete holds the record for the most Olympic appearances?

Answer: Austrian sailor Hubert Raudaschl, who competed in nine Olympic Games from 1964 to 1996.

Question: What is the record for the most consecutive games played in MLB?

Answer: Cal Ripken Jr., who played in 2,632 consecutive games.

Question: Who holds the record for the fastest 100 meter sprint in history?

Answer: Usain Bolt, with a time of 9.58 seconds set in 2009.

Question: What is the highest individual score in a single inning of a Major League Baseball game?

Answer: Wilbert Robinson holds the record with a 7-hit game in 1892, during which he scored 11 runs.

Music and Music History

Could you imagine Rock & Roll, without the electric guitar? Well, neither could Adolf Rickenbacker.

Adolph Rickenbacker's pivotal role in the invention of the electric guitar marks a transformative moment in the history of music, blending innovation with craftsmanship to reshape the sound and possibilities of modern instruments.

Born out of the need to amplify the guitar's sound in noisy band environments of the 1920s and 30s, Rickenbacker, along with his partner George Beauchamp, embarked on a journey that would forever change music. Their collaboration led to the creation of the first commercially successful electric guitar, the "Frying Pan," in 1931. Named for its round, skillet-like body, the Frying Pan featured a unique electromagnetic pickup that converted string vibrations into electrical signals, allowing them to be amplified through an external amplifier.

This breakthrough not only addressed practical issues of volume and projection but also unleashed a new realm of sonic possibilities. Musicians could now experiment with tone, sustain, and effects previously unattainable with acoustic instruments alone. The electric guitar quickly gained popularity among jazz, blues, and later rock musicians, becoming synonymous with the sound of modern popular music.

Rickenbacker's contributions extended beyond mere innovation; they represented a fusion of engineering ingenuity and artistic expression. By bridging the gap between instrument design and electrical engineering, Rickenbacker laid the foundation for subsequent advancements in guitar technology, paving the way for iconic instruments and legendary musicians who defined generations.

Beyond its technical merits, the electric guitar symbolizes a cultural shift, empowering musicians to push boundaries and redefine genres. It embodies the spirit of innovation and creativity that continues to resonate through music today, reminding us of the profound impact one invention can have on shaping the course of musical history.

The Rock & Roll Hall of Fame considers guitarists Jimi Hendrix, Eric Clapton, Jimmy Page, and Eddie Van Halen among the greatest of all time.

And speaking of great guitars…

The Fender Stratocaster, affectionately known as the "Strat," emerged in 1954 as a bold departure from its predecessors, the Telecaster and the Esquire. Designed by Leo Fender and his team in Fullerton, California, the Stratocaster was a marvel of modern design and functionality, embodying the spirit of the burgeoning electric guitar revolution.

Its sleek, contoured double-cutaway body, crafted from solid ash or alder, represented a departure from the more traditional guitar shapes of its time. This ergonomic design not only enhanced comfort but also facilitated greater access to the higher frets, enabling guitarists to explore new sonic territories with ease.

Equally revolutionary were its electronics. The Stratocaster boasted three single-coil pickups, strategically positioned to capture a wide spectrum of tones. This setup offered players unparalleled versatility, from the sparkling clean tones favored by surf rock pioneers to the gritty, overdriven sounds that defined the blues and rock 'n' roll eras.

One of the most distinctive features of the Stratocaster was its synchronized tremolo system, often referred to as the "whammy bar." This tremolo allowed players to manipulate pitch and create shimmering vibrato effects, adding a dynamic dimension to their playing style. Combined with the smooth action of its bolt-on maple neck and the iconic Fender headstock, the Stratocaster quickly became a favorite among musicians seeking innovation and expression.

Over the decades, the Stratocaster has evolved while maintaining its core essence. It has been wielded by legends such as Jimi Hendrix, Eric Clapton, and Stevie Ray Vaughan, each leaving an indelible mark on music history with their distinct interpretations of its sonic capabilities.

Today, the Fender Stratocaster remains an enduring symbol of creativity and craftsmanship. Its timeless design and versatile sound continue to inspire generations of guitarists, cementing its place as one of the most iconic and beloved electric guitars ever created.

For a great example of the Strat in action, search on YouTube for David Gilmour playing the Fender Stratocaster. I personally enjoy the Fender 50th Anniversary video of David Gilmour (Pink Floyd).

Shortly before The Beatles became a worldwide sensation, their original drummer, Randolph Peter Best, was replaced by Ringo Starr.

Ringo Starr's drumming style is celebrated for its simplicity, groove, and innate sense of musicality. Eschewing flashy techniques, he anchored The Beatles' sound with impeccable timing and a knack for enhancing each song's feel. His signature beats, like the iconic intro to "Come Together" or the steady pulse of "A Hard Day's Night," showcased his ability to serve the song rather than showcase his prowess.

Ringo's understated fills and solid backbeat became integral to the band's sound, influencing countless drummers and proving that sometimes, less is more in the art of rhythm.

Legend has it that Wolfgang Amadeus Mozart, known for his prodigious talent and playful personality, once found himself in a peculiar predicament during a visit to Vienna. While attending a lavish banquet hosted by a wealthy patron, Mozart, renowned for his wit, engaged in a friendly musical duel with another esteemed composer of the time.

As the evening wore on and the conversation turned to music, Mozart, never one to resist a musical challenge, proposed a spontaneous improvisation contest. With an ornate harpsichord at his disposal, Mozart dazzled the assembled guests with his virtuosity, weaving intricate melodies and lightning-fast passages with effortless grace.

However, the climax of the evening came when Mozart, known for his mischievous streak, playfully incorporated snippets of popular Viennese folk tunes into his improvisations. This unexpected twist delighted the audience and earned him admiration not only for his technical prowess but also for his ability to infuse classical music with a touch of humor and local flavor.

The anecdote captures Mozart's charm, musical brilliance, and his unique ability to captivate audiences both with his technical skill and his playful creativity.

In the final years of his life, Ludwig van Beethoven embarked on a monumental task: composing his Ninth Symphony, a work that would redefine the symphonic genre. Despite his increasing deafness, Beethoven poured his soul into this masterpiece, aiming to break new ground in both scale and emotional depth.

During rehearsals for the premiere in Vienna, Beethoven, now completely deaf, stood before the orchestra, conducting with passionate gestures that only he could hear in his mind. The symphony's unconventional structure, including the inclusion of vocal soloists and a chorus in the final movement, perplexed some musicians and critics alike.

However, during the premiere performance in 1824, as the symphony's triumphant finale, the "Ode to Joy," swelled to its climax, Beethoven, still conducting with fervor, was unaware of the roaring applause that erupted from the audience. It wasn't until one of the soloists gently turned him around to face the crowd that he saw the standing ovation he had received.

Beethoven's Ninth Symphony transcended its time, becoming a symbol of human resilience and the power of music to communicate profound emotion and universal truths, forever cementing its place as one of the greatest achievements in Western classical music.

Shifting from classic music to an iconic mid 20th century legend…

Hank Williams, the iconic country music legend, was known for his raw emotion and ability to capture the essence of human experience in his songs. One lesser-known anecdote from his early career highlights his determination and passion for music.

In the late 1930s, before fame found him, Hank Williams was struggling to make ends meet while performing at small venues across Alabama. One stormy night, he arrived at a local honky-tonk to find only a handful of patrons braving the weather. Undeterred, Hank took to the stage with his guitar and poured his heart into each song, despite the sparse audience.

Halfway through his set, the power suddenly went out, plunging the honky-tonk into darkness. Without missing a beat, Hank continued to sing and strum his guitar, the sound of his voice echoing through the room. The patrons, moved by his dedication and talent, lit matches and candles to illuminate the stage, creating an intimate atmosphere that intensified the emotional impact of his music.

This moment, though humble and unscripted, encapsulated Hank Williams' spirit: a relentless dedication to his craft and an innate ability to connect with listeners through the power of his songs.

Hank Williams passed away tragically on New Year's Day, 1953, at the age of 29. His death, attributed to heart failure exacerbated by years of substance abuse, marked the premature end of a country music icon whose timeless songs continue to resonate with audiences worldwide.

Following in Hank Williams' footsteps, George Jones gained an early reputation for drinking and missing concerts. So much so, his nickname was once, No Show Jones. Despite that, he electrified his country music fans.

George Jones, born on September 12, 1931, in Saratoga, Texas, rose to fame as one of the most influential voices in country music. Known for his distinctive baritone and emotive delivery, Jones recorded numerous hits including "He Stopped Loving Her Today," considered one of the greatest country songs. His tumultuous personal life, marked by struggles with alcohol and tumultuous relationships, often mirrored in his music, added depth to his songs.

Despite personal challenges, Jones' talent earned him accolades, including Grammy Awards and induction into the Country Music Hall of Fame. His legacy endures through his unparalleled vocal style and enduring impact on the genre, solidifying his place as a true country music legend.

During World War II, many of th etop celebrities and musicians of the itme travelled with the USO performing shows for servicemembers around the world. Among those was a family of young ladies known as the Andrew Sisters.

The Andrews Sisters, consisting of LaVerne, Maxene, and Patty Andrews, became iconic figures in the swing and pop music scenes of the 1930s and 1940s. Known for their tight harmonies and infectious energy, they achieved widespread fame with hits like "Boogie Woogie Bugle Boy" and "Rum and Coca-Cola."

During World War II, their music played a crucial role in boosting morale among Allied troops. The Andrews Sisters performed tirelessly at USO shows, military bases, and war bond rallies, entertaining soldiers with their lively performances and uplifting songs. Their blend of swing, boogie-woogie, and patriotic tunes resonated deeply with servicemen and women overseas, providing a comforting reminder of home amidst the hardships of war.

Their contributions to wartime morale earned them admiration and gratitude from both military personnel and civilians alike, solidifying their legacy as not only talented entertainers but also as vital morale boosters during one of the most challenging periods in modern history.

In the 1950s and 1960s, soul music emerged as a powerful cultural force in America, blending elements of gospel, rhythm and blues, and jazz into a dynamic new sound. Artists like Ray Charles, Aretha Franklin, and James Brown led the charge, infusing their music with raw emotion and social commentary.

An iconic moment in soul music's rise came in 1967 when Aretha Franklin released "Respect." Originally written and performed by Otis Redding, Franklin's rendition transformed the song into a feminist anthem and a rallying cry for civil rights. Its energetic rhythm, soulful vocals, and empowering lyrics resonated deeply across racial and social divides, catapulting

Franklin to fame and solidifying soul music's place as a voice for empowerment and cultural change in America.

The Motown sound refers to a distinctive style of music that originated from Motown Records, a record label founded by Berry Gordy Jr. in Detroit, Michigan, in 1959. Characterized by its rhythmic drive, catchy melodies, and polished production, the Motown sound blended elements of rhythm and blues, gospel, and pop music.

Key features of the Motown sound included tight vocal harmonies, often performed by groups like The Temptations and The Supremes, accompanied by upbeat rhythms provided by the label's house band, The Funk Brothers. The use of catchy hooks, sophisticated arrangements, and a focus on creating radio-friendly hits contributed to Motown's commercial success and cultural impact.

Motown artists such as Marvin Gaye, Stevie Wonder, and The Jackson 5 achieved international acclaim during the 1960s and 1970s, with their music transcending racial barriers and influencing generations of musicians. The Motown sound remains a defining chapter in the history of popular music, celebrated for its innovation, soulful performances, and lasting influence on the music industry.

Elvis Presley, born on January 8, 1935, in Tupelo, Mississippi, grew up immersed in the rich musical traditions of the American South. Influenced deeply by black spiritual music, Elvis's exposure to gospel singers at church and local radio stations left an indelible mark on his musical style.

In his formative years, Elvis was particularly drawn to the powerful, emotive vocals and rhythmic cadences of African American gospel music. He admired artists like Sister Rosetta Tharpe and Mahalia Jackson, whose soul-stirring performances resonated with him. Their influence shaped Elvis's vocal delivery, infusing his own singing with passion and intensity.

This fusion of gospel, blues, and country elements became a hallmark of Elvis's distinctive sound. It propelled him to fame in the 1950s, where his dynamic stage presence and groundbreaking rock 'n' roll hits like "Hound Dog" and "Heartbreak Hotel" captivated audiences worldwide. Elvis's ability to blend genres and incorporate spiritual influences not only revolutionized popular music but also bridged cultural divides, leaving an enduring legacy that continues to inspire generations of musicians.

In the mid-1950s, the rise of rock and roll ignited a cultural revolution, blending rhythm and blues with country and gospel influences to create a vibrant new sound. One iconic moment epitomizing this era occurred in 1956 when Elvis Presley's electrifying performance of "Hound Dog" on The Ed Sullivan Show captivated a national audience. His provocative dance moves and raw vocal energy sparked both frenzy and controversy, symbolizing a generational shift in music and youth culture.

Simultaneously, artists like Chuck Berry, Little Richard, and Buddy Holly emerged, each contributing their unique styles to the burgeoning genre. Their songs, filled with infectious beats and rebellious lyrics, resonated with young audiences hungry for something fresh and exciting. This fusion of musical innovation and cultural rebellion laid the foundation for rock and roll's enduring legacy, challenging societal norms and setting the stage for decades of musical evolution and influence.

• ▬▬▬▬▬ • • ▬▬▬▬▬ •

In the 1960s, rock and roll underwent a transformative evolution, shaped by a diverse array of influential artists who pushed musical boundaries and defined the decade's sound.

The Beatles, hailing from Liverpool, England, revolutionized rock with their infectious melodies, innovative songwriting, and charismatic stage presence. Their albums like "Sgt. Pepper's Lonely Hearts Club Band" showcased experimental production techniques and eclectic musical influences, setting new standards for creativity in popular music.

The Rolling Stones, known for their raw, blues-infused rock sound, emerged as rebellious counterparts to The Beatles. Led by Mick Jagger and Keith Richards, they brought gritty authenticity and dynamic stage performances to the forefront of rock culture.

Meanwhile, in the United States, artists like Bob Dylan pioneered folk rock, blending socially conscious lyrics with acoustic instrumentation. Dylan's introspective songwriting and poetic lyrics influenced a generation of musicians and expanded the lyrical possibilities of rock music.

Jimi Hendrix, with his virtuosic guitar playing and psychedelic soundscapes, redefined the electric guitar's role in rock music, while The Beach Boys innovated with intricate vocal harmonies and sophisticated production techniques.

Collectively, these artists and others like The Who, The Doors, and Aretha Franklin not only shaped the sound of the 1960s but also laid the groundwork for the diverse genres and subgenres that continue to define rock and roll today.

•▰▰▰▰▰▰▰• •▰▰▰▰▰▰•

In the 1970s, disco music emerged as a cultural phenomenon, characterized by its pulsating beats, lush orchestration, and emphasis on danceable rhythms. Several key influencers shaped the disco movement, leaving an indelible mark on music and popular culture.

The Bee Gees, originally a pop-rock band, reinvented themselves with a string of disco hits like "Stayin' Alive" and "Night Fever." Their falsetto harmonies and catchy melodies became synonymous with the disco sound, catapulting them to global superstardom.

Donna Summer, known as the "Queen of Disco," brought a powerful voice and sensual charisma to the genre. Hits like "Love to Love You Baby" and "Hot Stuff" showcased her dynamic vocal range and helped define disco's sultry and glamorous aesthetic.

Chic, led by Nile Rodgers and Bernard Edwards, pioneered a sophisticated blend of funk and disco with songs like "Le Freak" and "Good Times," influencing both the dance floor and future genres like hip-hop.

Studio 54, the legendary New York City nightclub, served as a hub for disco culture, attracting celebrities and dancers who embraced its hedonistic spirit and glamorous fashion.

Collectively, these influencers and others like KC and the Sunshine Band, Gloria Gaynor, and Village People propelled disco music to unprecedented popularity, transforming it into a

140

global phenomenon that continues to influence dance music and popular culture today.

<hr>

Woodstock, held from August 15-18, 1969, in Bethel, New York, remains an iconic symbol of the 1960s counterculture and a pivotal moment in music history. Conceived as "An Aquarian Exposition: 3 Days of Peace & Music," the festival attracted an estimated 400,000 attendees, surpassing all expectations.

The lineup featured legendary artists spanning rock, folk, blues, and psychedelic genres, including Jimi Hendrix, The Who, Janis Joplin, Santana, and Crosby, Stills, Nash & Young. Despite logistical challenges and adverse weather conditions, the event unfolded peacefully, fueled by a spirit of communal harmony and artistic expression.

Woodstock became a cultural touchstone, symbolizing youth rebellion, anti-war sentiment, and the quest for social change. It highlighted the power of music to unite and inspire, leaving a lasting legacy of idealism and creative freedom. The Woodstock Festival not only defined a generation but also set a precedent for future music festivals as platforms for cultural revolution and musical innovation.

<hr>

Taylor Swift is a globally renowned singer-songwriter who first gained prominence in the mid-2000s for her country-pop music. Born on December 13, 1989, in Pennsylvania, Swift moved to Nashville, Tennessee, to pursue a career in country music and released her debut album, "Taylor Swift," in 2006. Her early success was marked by heartfelt lyrics, catchy melodies, and relatable storytelling that resonated with audiences of all ages.

Swift's popularity soared with subsequent albums like "Fearless," "Speak Now," and "Red," where she expanded her musical style to include pop influences while maintaining her signature songwriting prowess. Her albums consistently topped charts, earning critical acclaim and numerous awards, including Grammy Awards and American Music Awards.

Beyond her music, Taylor Swift's personal authenticity, advocacy for artists' rights, and connection with fans through social media have contributed to her enduring popularity. She has successfully navigated transitions in musical genres and maintained a loyal fan base, making her one of the most influential and commercially successful artists of her generation.

Random Q & A

Question: What two songs recorded by the Beatles were written exclusively by Ringo Starr?

Answer: *Octopus's Garden* and *Don't Pass Me By*.

Other songs with Ringo Starr's name in the credits include *What Goes On*, *Maggie Mae*, *Dig It*, and *Flying*.

Question: What is the band known as The Who?

Answer: The Who is an English rock band that was formed in 1962. Their original group name was The Detours.

From 1964 to 1978, the band included Roger Daltry, Pete Townshend, John Entwistle, and Keith Moon.

The Who is recognized as one of the most influential rock bands in history, and have sold over 100 million albums worldwide. They were inducted into the Rock and Roll Hall of Fame in 1990.

Tragedy struck the band on 3 December 1979, when a crowd of concert goers rushed the Riverfront Coliseum doors in Cincinnati, Ohio. 11 people were crushed to death. According to the organizers, concert seating was first come, first served, resulting in a mad dash for the doors when the crowd heard the band testing its sound system.

The Beatles enjoyed The Who, and Paul McCartney claims the group inspired their song, *Helter Skelter*. Interestingly, the leader of the Manson Family, Charles Manson, believed the *Helter Skelter* album revealed hidden messages to him.

Question: What is Micky Dolenz famous for?

Answer: Drummer for the Monkees.

At the time Dolenz was recruited to play the drums for the Monkees, he did not known how to play the drums.

Dolenz was however a good mime. Tutors taught him how to fake playing the drums. Over time, Dolenz learned how to play the drums well enough to tour with the Monkees and perform live shows.

Question: Who was known as the "King of Pop"?

Answer: Michael Jackson. Born in 1958, Michael Jackson rose to fame as a child prodigy with the Jackson 5 before launching a wildly successful solo career. His album *Thriller* remains the best-selling album of all time, and his influence on pop music and dance is unparalleled.

Question: Which rock band was famously formed in Liverpool, England, in 1960?

Answer: The Beatles. The four man band included John Lennon, Paul McCartney, George Harrison, and Ringo Starr. Shortly after the band was formed, drummer Ringo Starr replaced the original drummer, Randolph Peter Best.

The Beatles revolutionized popular music and became one of the most influential bands in history. Their impact on culture and music resonates to this day.

Question: What was the first music video ever played on MTV when it launched in 1981?

Answer: *Video Killed the Radio Star* by The Buggles. This catchy synth-pop track became iconic as the inaugural video on MTV, symbolizing the dawn of a new era in music consumption.

Question: Who is often credited with inventing the electric guitar?

Answer: Les Paul.

Paul is also known for his contributions to multitrack recording techniques.

Question: What iconic festival hosted over 400,000 attendees in 1969, featuring legendary performances by Jimi Hendrix, Janis Joplin, and The Who?

Answer: Woodstock. Held in upstate New York, Woodstock has become synonymous with the counterculture movement of the 1960s and remains one of the most celebrated music festivals in history.

Question: Which female artist holds the record for the most number-one singles on the Billboard Hot 100 chart?

Answer: Mariah Carey.

Question: What influential punk band released their self-titled debut album in 1977, featuring tracks like *Anarchy in the U.K.?*

Answer: Sex Pistols. Heralded as one of the pioneers of the punk rock movement, the Sex Pistols shocked and captivated audiences with their raw energy and rebellious attitude.

Question: Which album by Pink Floyd spent a record-breaking 741 weeks on the Billboard 200 chart?

Answer: *The Dark Side of the Moon*, released in 1973.

Question: Who was the lead singer of the influential grunge band Nirvana?

Answer: Kurt Cobain.

Question: What famous venue did Elvis Presley famously headline in his 1968 comeback special?

Answer: The International Hotel in Las Vegas.

Question: Who wrote the classic song *Imagine,* which became an anthem for peace and unity?

Answer: John Lennon. Released in 1971.

Question: What music genre originated in Jamaica in the late 1960s, characterized by its offbeat rhythms and socially conscious lyrics?

Answer: Reggae. Popularized by artists like Bob Marley and The Wailers.

Question: What was the name of the recording studio in Memphis, Tennessee, where artists like Elvis Presley and Johnny Cash recorded some of their most famous tracks?

Answer: Sun Studio. Often referred to as the "Birthplace of Rock 'n' Roll."

Question: Who famously performed the guitar solo on Michael Jackson's hit song *Beat It*?

Answer: Eddie Van Halen.

Question: What iconic music festival took place in 1967 in San Francisco's Golden Gate Park, featuring performances by Jefferson Airplane, The Grateful Dead, and Janis Joplin?

Answer: The Monterey Pop Festival.

Question: What singer-songwriter released the critically acclaimed album *Blue* in 1971, known for its introspective lyrics and emotional depth?

Answer: Joni Mitchell.

Question: What iconic rock band's 1971 hit *Stairway to Heaven* is often regarded as one of the greatest rock songs of all time?

Answer: Led Zeppelin. The Led Zeppelin band included vocalist Robert Plant, guitarist Jimmy Page, bassist and keyboardist John Paul Jones, and drummer John Bonham.

Question: What legendary singer-songwriter was awarded the Nobel Prize in Literature in 2016 for his poetic contributions to music?

Answer: Bob Dylan.

Question: What was the first music video ever played on MTV Europe when it launched in 1987?

Answer: *Money for Nothing* by Dire Straits.

Question: What iconic dance move was popularized by James Brown in the 1960s?

Answer: The "James Brown Shuffle."

This section obviously barely scratches the surface on music history and the amazing people who create it. To learn more music trivia, please consider my other trivia book, *Massive Rock Band Trivia*.

Film and Television

A popular trivia game challenges players to find connections between movies, actors, writers, and directors, where a player introduces a movie or name and challenges the other player to name a movie or name that is somehow connected. As the game goes on, the players can find themselves lost in a rabbit warren of connections.

For example, the 1977 movie, *The Duelists*, presents a plethora of connections. The director, Ridley Scott, is also famous for directing *Alien*, *Blade Runner*, and *Thelma & Louise*, among many others. The key role in *The Duelists* is played by Keith Carradine, whose brother played the main role of Grasshopper, in the television series *Kung Fu*. At that time in Hollywood, producers were hesitant to cast actual Chinese to play Chinese roles, despite Bruce Lee's amazing performance in *The Green Hornet* television show as Kato. *The Duelists* was based on a story by Joseph Conrad, who also wrote the book, *Heart of Darkness*, which inspired the movie, *Apocalypse Now*.

As you can see, a bit of movie and television trivia knowledge could lead to hours of entertainment.

Have you ever heard of Daisy Dukes? The expression is proof that sitcoms, movies, music, and literature do impact society at large, including culture.

The expression Daisy dukes comes from a popular television series, *The Dukes of Hazzard*.

The Dukes of Hazzard comedic drama, also known as a dramedy, first aired on CBS television on 26 January 1979. It lasted until 8 February 1985, and produced 147 episodes. The show was created by Gy Waldron, and was inspired by a 1975 movie called *Moonrunners*, also created by Gy Waldron, with the technical assistance of an alleged moonshiner named Jerry Rushing.

Considered the second most popular television show of its time, it ranked one notch below another CBS hit show called *Dallas*, with Larry Hagman in the role of J.R. Ewing.

The basic plot behind *The Dukes of Hazzard* revolves around two country boys from Georgia who have a history of running moonshine. In an effort to expose the corruption of their county commissioner Boss Hogg and county sheriff, Rosco Coltrane, the cousins devise different schemes to evade the law while continuing to ply their illicit trade.

Their preferred method of evasion is to outrun the law in their 1969 Dodge Charger, named General Lee.

One of the more memorable characters in the show is yet another cousin, named Daisy Duke. Daisy is famous for wearing extremely short hot pants, made from cutoff denim jeans and known to this day as Daisy Dukes.

Long before Daisy Duke titillated viewers with her Daisy Dukes, Mary Ann, played by former Miss Nevada Dawn Wells, from *Gilligan's Island,* spent virtually every minute of her time on air prancing around in a tight pair of shorts.

Interestingly, broadcast television censors at the time thought Mary Ann's tight shorts were too revealing, and required the top of her shorts extend upward, past her navel.

Gilligan's Island first aired on 26 September 1964 on CBS. The last episode aired on 17 April 1967, for a total of 98 episodes. Over the years, *Gilligan's Island* has remained one of the most popular reruns in television history.

The cast included Bob Denver as Gilligan, Alan Hale as the Skipper, Jim Backus as Thurston Howell III, Natalie Schafer as Eunice "Lovey" Howell, Tina Louise as Ginger Grant, Russell Johnson as Professor Roy Hinkley, and Dawn Wells as Mary Ann Summers

Mary Ann seems out of place with millionaires, movie stars, and college professors. According to character bios, Mary Ann is a farm girl from Winfield, Kansas. She had won the trip and the boat tour in a lottery. Lucky her. And while the show makes a big deal about the glamorous beauty of Ginger, show producers were surprised to discover the vast majority of male viewers found the "girl next door" looks of Mary Ann more attractive than Ginger.

Finally, fans of *Gilligan's Island* may be familiar with scenes featuring random radio broadcasts. The voice actor on the radio was played by Charles Maxwell.

Gilligan's Island was filmed at Studio City, Los Angeles, and used part of the parking lot to build a lagoon. The opening scenes portraying the *Minnow* leaving the harbor were filmed in Hawaii.

Tragically, the last day of filming the pilot episode was 22 November 1963, the date of Kennedy's assassination. In some of the opening sequences of *Gilligan's Island*, a flag set at half mast can be seen.

⬥▰▰▰▰⬥ ⬥▰▰▰▰⬥

The original sitcom TV series, *Happy Days*, featured a middle class American family in the late 1950s and early 1960s, with a particular focus on the lifestyles, challenges, and cultural norms of teen life at the time.

The first *Happy Days* episode aired on ABC on 15 January 1974. The show ran 11 seasons, and aired 255 half hour episodes. The final episode aired on 19 July 1984.

Prior to being a hit TV show, *Happy Days* was portrayed as a sketch on another show from 1972 called, *Love American Style*. And then in 1973 George Lucas directed a film called *American Graffiti*, featuring Ron Howard as a 1950s teenager. ABC took note of the public interest in the movie and decided to green light production of the TV show.

Fans of the *Happy Days* show may remember the main character, Richie Cunningham, was played by a teenaged Ron Howard, while an older friend of Richie named Fonzie, or The Fonz, was played by Henry Winkler. The Fonz was a cool mentor type guy, who of course rode a motorcycle and constantly combed his hair.

The main cast for *Happy Days* included Ron Howard as Richie Cunningham, Henry Winkler as Fonzie, and Tom Bosley and

Marion Ross as Richie's parents, Howard and Marion Cunningham.

John Travolta and George "Micky" Dolenz from the *Monkees* auditioned for the role of The Fonz before the producers settled on Henry Wnkler. As it turns out, both Dolenz and Travolta were much taller than the other cast members, making pairing the actors on screen awkward.

Travolta went on to create an amazing acting, singing, and dancing career in the hit TV show, *Welcome Back Kotter*, followed by leading movie roles in *Grease* and *Saturday Night Fever*.

Interestingly, Henry Winkler was asked to audition for Travolta's role in *Grease*, but turned it down due to his self-described inability to carry a tune.

The first television show ever broadcast depends on the definition of "television show." In terms of experimental broadcasts and public demonstrations, the first widely recognized event was the transmission of a ventriloquist's dummy named "Stooky Bill" in 1925 by John Logie Baird in London. However, the first regular, scheduled television service began in the United Kingdom by the BBC in 1936, which included programming such as variety shows, dramas, and documentaries. Therefore, while "Stooky Bill" was the first broadcast, the BBC's regular programming in 1936 marked the beginning of what we now consider scheduled television shows.

Years later, shows like *The Honeymooners* and *The Howdy Doody* show entertained Americans. Howdy Doody was especially popular with children.

"The Howdy Doody Show," airing from 1947 to 1960, was an iconic children's television program featuring Buffalo Bob Smith and his puppet Howdy Doody. It blended comedy, music, and audience participation, becoming a beloved fixture of early TV. The show's characters and catchphrases remain nostalgic touchstones for many viewers.

The invention of television was a culmination of scientific discoveries and technological advancements spanning several decades. Key milestones include:

- Early Experiments: In the late 19th and early 20th centuries, inventors like Paul Nipkow, John Logie Baird, and Vladimir Zworykin developed crucial components such as the Nipkow disk (1884) and cathode ray tube (CRT).

- Mechanical Television: Baird demonstrated the first working mechanical television system in 1925, using a rotating disk with holes to transmit images.

- Electronic Television: Zworykin's development of the iconoscope and kinescope in the 1920s paved the way for electronic television, which used electronic scanning and display methods.

- First Broadcasts: The first public television broadcasts occurred in the 1920s and 1930s, with experimental broadcasts by Baird in the UK and by RCA in the US.

- Commercialization: Regular television broadcasting began in the late 1930s, with the BBC launching regular services in 1936 and NBC starting regular broadcasts in the US in 1939.

- Post-War Expansion: After World War II, television technology rapidly evolved, with improvements in picture quality, programming diversity, and the adoption of color television in the 1950s.

Television's invention revolutionized communication and entertainment, shaping modern culture and becoming a ubiquitous medium worldwide.

The first live broadcast on television is attributed to several events, each marking significant milestones in television history:

- Felix the Cat: In 1928, Charles Francis Jenkins demonstrated the first successful live broadcast of a television image in the United States. The image transmitted was of Felix the Cat, a popular cartoon character.

- 1936 Berlin Olympics: The 1936 Summer Olympics in Berlin marked the first live television broadcast of a major sporting event. The German broadcasting service (Reichs-Rundfunk-Gesellschaft) transmitted live coverage of events to specially equipped viewing rooms.

- 1936 BBC Television Service: The BBC initiated the world's first regular public television service in November 1936. The opening night featured live broadcasts, including performances, interviews, and news updates.

- 1947 World Series: In the United States, the first live coast-to-coast television broadcast occurred during the 1947 World Series between the New York Yankees and the Brooklyn Dodgers, marking a pivotal moment in the growth of television as a mass medium.

These events laid the foundation for the live broadcasting techniques and technologies that continue to shape television production and viewership today.

Random Q & A

Question: What country music star played the rival football coach in the 1998 sports comedy film The Waterboy?

Answer: Jerry Reed played the rival football coach. The film also included Adam Sandler, Kathy Bates, and Henry Winkler.

Sandler's girlfriend was played by Fairuza Balk as Vicki Vallencourt.

Some of Jerry Reed's country music hits include: When You're Hot, You're Hot, Guitar Man, and East Bound and Down.

Question: What 1994 film stars Tim Robbins as Andy Dufresne, a man who is wrongfully imprisoned for the murder of his wife?

Answer: The Shawshank Redemption

Question: In the TV series "Friends," what is the name of Ross Geller's second wife?

Answer: Emily

Question: Who directed the 1972 movie "The Godfather"?

Answer: Francis Ford Coppola

Question: Which actor plays the character of Jack Dawson in "Titanic"?

Answer: Leonardo DiCaprio

Question: What is the highest-grossing animated film of all time as of 2023?

Answer: The Lion King (2019)

Question: In "Breaking Bad," what is Walter White's alias in the drug world?

Answer: Heisenberg

Question: What year was the original "Jurassic Park" film released?

Answer: 1993

Question: Who played the character of Forrest Gump in the 1994 film of the same name?

Answer: Tom Hanks

Question: Which TV show features a high school chemistry teacher turned methamphetamine manufacturer?

Answer: Breaking Bad

Question: What is the name of the fictional African country where "Black Panther" is set?

Answer: Wakanda

Question: In the movie "The Matrix," what is the name of the protagonist played by Keanu Reeves?

Answer: Neo

Question: Who is the female lead in the movie "La La Land"?

Answer: Emma Stone

Question: What long-running TV show is centered around the lives of doctors and nurses at the fictional Seattle Grace Hospital?

Answer: Grey's Anatomy

Question: What 1999 film featured the line, "I see dead people"?

Answer: The Sixth Sense

Question: Who directed "Inception"?

Answer: Christopher Nolan

Question: Which actor plays the title character in the TV show "Luther"?

Answer: Idris Elba

Question: What is the name of the dragon in the movie "How to Train Your Dragon"?

Answer: Toothless

Question: In "The Office," what is the name of the company where the characters work?

Answer: Dunder Mifflin

Question: Who won the Academy Award for Best Actor for his role in "Joker" (2019)?

Answer: Joaquin Phoenix

Question: Which film features the song "My Heart Will Go On"?

Answer: Titanic

Question: What TV show features a character named Sheldon Cooper?

Answer: The Big Bang Theory

Question: Who directed the 1994 film "Pulp Fiction"?

Answer: Quentin Tarantino

Question: What is the highest-grossing film of all time as of 2023?

Answer: Avatar

Question: In "Harry Potter," what is the name of Harry's owl?

Answer: Hedwig

Question: What TV series is known for the phrase "Winter is coming"?

Answer: Game of Thrones

Question: Who played the character of Tony Stark in the Marvel Cinematic Universe?

Answer: Robert Downey Jr.

Question: Which 1997 film was the first animated feature to be nominated for the Academy Award for Best Picture?

Answer: Beauty and the Beast

Question: In the TV show "Stranger Things," what is the name of the girl with telekinetic powers?

Answer: Eleven

Question: Who directed the "Lord of the Rings" trilogy?

Answer: Peter Jackson

Question: What film features a giant ape climbing the Empire State Building?

Answer: King Kong

Question: Who plays the character of Jon Snow in "Game of Thrones"?

Answer: Kit Harington

Question: What is the name of the main protagonist in the "Toy Story" series?

Answer: Woody

Question: What TV show is set in the fictional town of Pawnee, Indiana?

Answer: Parks and Recreation

Question: Who directed the 2013 film "Gravity"?

Answer: Alfonso Cuarón

Question: What is the name of the coffee shop where the characters in "Friends" often hang out?

Answer: Central Perk

Question: Who played the character of Katniss Everdeen in "The Hunger Games" series?

Answer: Jennifer Lawrence

Question: In the TV show "The Simpsons," what is the name of Bart Simpson's father?

Answer: Homer Simpson

Question: Who directed the film "E.T. the Extra-Terrestrial"?

Answer: Steven Spielberg

Question: What TV show features the character Daenerys Targaryen?

Answer: Game of Thrones

Question: Who starred as the titular character in the 2004 film "The Phantom of the Opera"?

Answer: Gerard Butler

Question: What is the name of the fictional school in the "X-Men" series?

Answer: Xavier's School for Gifted Youngsters

Question: In the TV show "Breaking Bad," what is the name of Jesse Pinkman's girlfriend who dies from an overdose?

Answer: Jane Margolis

Question: Who directed the 2008 film "The Dark Knight"?

Answer: Christopher Nolan

Question: What is the name of the kingdom where the movie "Frozen" is set?

Answer: Arendelle

Question: Who played the character of James Bond in the film "Skyfall"?

Answer: Daniel Craig

Question: What TV show is known for the phrase "Live long and prosper"?

Answer: Star Trek

Question: In "Harry Potter," who is the headmaster of Hogwarts during Harry's first year?

Answer: Albus Dumbledore

Question: Who played the character of Rick Blaine in "Casablanca"?

Answer: Humphrey Bogart

Question: What TV show features the character of Olivia Pope?

Answer: Scandal

Question: Who directed the 1993 film "Schindler's List"?

Answer: Steven Spielberg

Question: In "The Matrix," what is the name of the ship captained by Morpheus?

Answer: Nebuchadnezzar

Question: Who plays the character of Michael Scott in "The Office"?

Answer: Steve Carell

Question: What is the name of the fictional continent where "Game of Thrones" is set?

Answer: Westeros

Question: In "Star Wars," who is the father of Luke Skywalker?

Answer: Darth Vader

Question: Who played the character of Elle Woods in "Legally Blonde"?

Answer: Reese Witherspoon

Question: What TV show follows the lives of the Fisher family who run a funeral home?

Answer: Six Feet Under

Question: Who directed the 2010 film "Black Swan"?

Answer: Darren Aronofsky

Question: In "Friends," what is the name of Joey's stuffed penguin?

Answer: Hugsy

Question: Who played the character of Maximus Decimus Meridius in "Gladiator"?

Answer: Russell Crowe

Question: What TV show is set on the fictional street of Wisteria Lane?

Answer: Desperate Housewives

Question: Who played Wednesday Addams in the Netflix adaptation of "Wednesday"?

Answer: Jenna Ortega

Question: What television series served as a prequel to the hit show "The Big Bang Theory"?

Answer: "Young Sheldon"

Technology and Innovation

Long before the Internet, email, text messages, radio, and even the telephone, you could either write a letter to your mother in Peoria and wait weeks for a response, or send a telegram over the wire using Morse code.

An American inventor and artist named Samuel Morse developed a means of communicating over a wire by sending an electric pulse over the wire. Varying the length of each pulse created an audible dot or dash, also known as a dit or dah.

Around 1847 Morse turned the ability to transmit and receive dits and dahs into a language of dots and dashes representing letters and numbers. Earliest uses of Morse code involved a teletype machine that punched holes into thin strips of paper according to received dits and dahs. It wasn't long before Wall Street capitalized on instant communication and adopted what came ot be known as Ticker Tape Machines.

Early in the development of Morse code and the rise in popularity of sending and receiving telegrams across the nation, companies like Western Union and the Grand Trunk Railway used railroad right-of-ways to string telegraph lines across the continent. Naturally, transmitting and receiving telegraphic messages fell to the railroad, where each station could operate a telegraph office to receive and pass on messages.

Around 1862 a 15 year old boy was taught how to send and receive telegrams, and by 1867 he was employed by the Grand Trunk Railway and made responsible for one of these train station telegram relay offices near Ontario, Canada.

A popular hazing, or initiation, tradition of the time was for experienced telegraph operators up and down the railway line to intentionally transmit messages in high speed, prompting the less experienced telegraph operator to ask for a resend, an embarrassing and humbling request by any self-respecting telegraph operator.

Weeks went by and the telegraph operators along the Grand Trunk Railway line noticed they were unable to trip up the newbie in Ontario. Curious, a telegraph operator dropped by to see what was gong on. When he found a boy named Thomas Edison leaning back in a chair while reading a book and transmitting Morse code with his toe, he knew the hazing was a waste of time.

In 1887 radio waves were discovered, and by 1899 the means to send and receive wireless telegraphic messages were developed, enabling ships at sea to communicate with each other and the shore.

By 1906 this technology led to the creation of a standard emergency transmission knows as SOS. While many people believe SOS stands for "Save Our Ship," or "Save Our Souls," in actuality, the letters SOS don't stand for anything. The SOS is a recognized emergency distress signal that uses three dots, three dashes, and three dots. An easily recognized and repeatable signal.

When the Titanic sank on 14 April 1912, the standard SOS was not widely known or accepted, and radio operators on the Titanic sent various distress signals, including the SOS signal. The conflicting messages created confusion and delayed rescue of the doomed Titanic. Sense then, SOS has come to be recognized as the one and only emergency distress signal utilizing Morse code.

With the development of voice capable radio reception and transmission, the more commonly used distress signal, "mayday, mayday, mayday," became the standard emergency distress signal around 1920.

The term was conceived of by a British radio operator named Frederick Stanley Mockford. Mockford worked a radio station at Croydon Airport, England. At the time, most aircraft traffic handled by the airport involved craft flying in from France. The word "mayady" was Mockford's interpretation of the words "m'aidez," which means "help me."

Jargon is a fancy word for language and acronyms specific to an industry or trade. Leading the pack in its love for all things jargon, is the military…a world unto its own.

The military loves to use acronyms and initialisms to abbreviate speech and text. An acronym is a series of letters that create a pronounceable word, for example, SNAFU. An initialism, on the other hand, is a series of letters that mean something to people within the trade, but do not spell out a word, such as FNG.

The following acronyms and initialisms spread the F word around like a crop duster spreads Agent Orange. Wherever you see the word, "freak," think the F word. It won't be spelled out here.

FNG: Freaking New Guy
SNAFU: Situation Normal All Freaked Up
FUBAR: Freaked Up Beyond All Recognition
BOHICA: Bend Over, Here It Comes Again
FISH: Fighting In Someone's House
CHIPS: Causing Havoc In Peoples Streets
FRED: Freaking Ridiculous Eating Device
SUSFU: Situation Unchanged Still Freaked Up
TARFU: Totally And Royally Freaked Up
REMF: Rear Echelon Mother Freaker
FOBBIT: Forward Operating Base Resident

The acronym FOBBIT is not entirely accurate and plays on the Tolkien name Hobbit to describe a soldier who is essentially in the rear with the gear, and not a soldier who goes outside the wire, or engages with the enemy. A deployed army designates small encampments or bases in the military area of operations as FOBs, or Forward Operating Bases.

Military operations also love the use of a phonetic alphabet to reduce miscommunication, typically over radio communications. For example, if a soldier, or police officer, transmitted a message spelling the name of a suspect, it would be easy to confuse the letter D with B, or N with M. Saying the phonetic name for a letter reduces the confusion.

NATO recognized phonetic alphabet:

A Alpha
B Bravo
C Charlie

D Delta
E Echo
F Foxtrot
G Golf
H Hotel
I India
J Juliett
K Kilo
L Lima
M Mike
N November
O Oscar
P Papa
Q Quebec
R Romeo
S Sierra
T Tango
U Uniform
V Victor
W Whiskey
X Xray
Y Yankee
Z Zulu

A 13th to 14th Century French theologian and philosopher named Durandus of Saint-Pourçain believed when all things are equal, the simplest explanation is generally the correct one. Shortly thereafter, another philosopher named William of Ockham postulated the same thing.

Apparently, William of Ockham had a better publicist, as his theory became known as Occam's Razor, a popular expression tossed around in conversations to this day, suggesting that if any situation or collection of alternatives poses an impossible decision, the easiest solution or idea is generally the best choice.

Random Q & A

Question: Who is known as the father of the modern computer?

Answer: Alan Turing

Question: What is the smallest unit of data in a computer?

Answer: Bit

Question: Which planet is known as the Red Planet?

Answer: Mars

Question: What does the acronym "NASA" stand for?

Answer: National Aeronautics and Space Administration

Question: Who invented the telephone?

Answer: Alexander Graham Bell

Question: What is the chemical symbol for gold?

Answer: Au

Question: Who is credited with the discovery of penicillin?

Answer: Alexander Fleming

Question: What does "HTML" stand for in web development?

Answer: HyperText Markup Language

Question: What is the name of the first artificial Earth satellite launched by the Soviet Union in 1957?

Answer: Sputnik

Question: What is the process of converting sunlight into electricity using semiconductors called?

Answer: Photovoltaic effect

Question: Who developed the theory of relativity?

Answer: Albert Einstein

Question: What does the acronym "DNA" stand for?

Answer: Deoxyribonucleic Acid

Question: What technology is used to make telephone calls over the Internet possible?

Answer: VoIP (Voice over Internet Protocol)

Question: Who invented the World Wide Web?

Answer: Tim Berners-Lee

Question: What is the name of the first programmable computer?

Answer: ENIAC (Electronic Numerical Integrator and Computer)

Question: Who is known for the laws of motion and universal gravitation?

Answer: Isaac Newton

Question: What is the main gas found in the Earth's atmosphere?

Answer: Nitrogen

Question: What does "HTTP" stand for?

Answer: HyperText Transfer Protocol

Question: Who is credited with the invention of the light bulb?

Answer: Thomas Edison

Question: What does the acronym "AI" stand for in technology?

Answer: Artificial Intelligence

Question: What element is the primary component of steel?

Answer: Iron

Question: Who was the first person to walk on the moon?

Answer: Neil Armstrong

Question: What does "RAM" stand for in computer terminology?

Answer: Random Access Memory

Question: Who invented the first successful airplane?

Answer: Wright brothers (Orville and Wilbur Wright)

Question: What is the study of living organisms called?

Answer: Biology

Question: What does "CPU" stand for?

Answer: Central Processing Unit

Question: What is the name of the first cloned sheep?

Answer: Dolly

Question: Who is credited with the invention of the first mechanical computer, the Analytical Engine?

Answer: Charles Babbage

Question: What is the chemical symbol for the element oxygen?

Answer: O

Question: What is the main language used to create Android apps?

Answer: Java

Question: Who developed the polio vaccine?

Answer: Jonas Salk

Question: What is the term for a network that covers a broad area, such as a city or campus?

Answer: MAN (Metropolitan Area Network)

Question: What is the name of the rover that landed on Mars in 2021?

Answer: Perseverance

Question: What is the process by which plants make their own food using sunlight called?

Answer: Photosynthesis

Question: Who is known for the discovery of radioactivity?

Answer: Marie Curie

Question: What does "URL" stand for?

Answer: Uniform Resource Locator

Question: Who is credited with the invention of the first practical telephone?

Answer: Alexander Graham Bell

Question: What is the name of the first electronic general-purpose computer?

Answer: ENIAC

Question: What is the chemical formula for water?

Answer: H_2O. H_2O stands for one molecule of hydrogen and two molecules of oxygen.

Question: What technology is used to read barcodes?

Answer: Barcode scanner

Question: Who proposed the heliocentric theory, which states that the Earth revolves around the Sun?

Answer: Nicolaus Copernicus

Question: What does "Wi-Fi" stand for?

Answer: Wireless Fidelity

Question: Who is known as the father of modern physics?

Answer: Albert Einstein

Question: What is the primary gas found on Jupiter?

Answer: Hydrogen

Question: Who is credited with the invention of the first practical automobile?

Answer: Karl Benz

Question: What does "VPN" stand for?

Answer: Virtual Private Network

Question: What is the closest star to Earth?

Answer: The Sun

Question: Who is known for the invention of the phonograph?

Answer: Thomas Edison

Question: What is the term for a disease that spreads across a large region or worldwide?

Answer: Pandemic

Question: What is the name of the programming language that is known for its simplicity and readability, often used for web development and data science?

Answer: Python

Question: What is the name of the first woman to win a Nobel Prize?

Answer: Marie Curie

Question: What does "SSD" stand for in computer storage?

Answer: Solid State Drive

Question: Who invented the first mechanical calculator?

Answer: Blaise Pascal

Question: What is the chemical symbol for helium?

Answer: He

Question: What is the name of the first spacecraft to reach interstellar space?

Answer: Voyager 1

Question: Who is credited with the discovery of the structure of DNA?

Answer: James Watson and Francis Crick

Question: What does "IoT" stand for?

Answer: Internet of Things

Question: What is the term for a device that converts digital signals into analog signals and vice versa?

Answer: Modem

Question: What is the name of the first human to journey into outer space?

Answer: Yuri Gagarin

Wining and Dining

As humans, we've elevated the act of eating and drinking to an art form, and throughout history, cultures around the globe have developed unique culinary traditions.

Whether you're a seasoned taste master or simply curious about the stories behind your favorite restaurants, dishes and beverages, prepare to tantalize your taste buds and expand your culinary knowledge with this broad selection of questions and answers relevant to food trivia.

The Golden Corral restaurant features an all-you-can-eat buffet with over 160 items, including a fan favorite chocolate fountain called Wonderfall. In various commercials, Golden Corral calls their chocolate fountain the 8th Wonder of the World.

With 489 locations across 41 states, Golden Corral has built its epicurean empire from a single steakhouse, opening on 3 January 1973. To join the franchise, an entrepreneur would need to pay a franchise fee of 2 to 7 million dollars, depending upon location and projected revenues.

Golden Corral was accused online of kicking a very hungry and well proportioned customer out of the restaurant after he reportedly ate 50 pounds worth of food. This story was eventually debunked as fake.

Emeril Lagasse, often recognized for his enthusiastic catchphrase "Bam!" and his energetic cooking style, has had a storied career that transcends the kitchen. One particular anecdote from his early years not only highlights his culinary prowess but also his dedication and flair for turning challenges into triumphs.

In the late 1980s, Emeril Lagasse was making a name for himself as the executive chef at the renowned Commander's Palace in New Orleans. Known for his innovative approach to Creole and Cajun cuisine, Emeril's charisma and talent were already setting him apart in the competitive culinary world.

One busy night, the restaurant was buzzing with patrons eager to experience Lagasse's culinary creations. Among the guests was a high-profile customer, a well-known food critic who had a reputation for being both discerning and difficult to please. As the orders flowed into the kitchen, Emeril received an unexpected and daunting request: the critic wanted a dish that wasn't on the menu—something entirely new and original, reflecting the essence of New Orleans but with a fresh twist.

Without missing a beat, Emeril sprang into action. He quickly scanned the pantry and refrigerators, his mind racing with possibilities. Drawing on his deep understanding of the local cuisine and his ability to improvise under pressure, he decided to create a unique dish combining local ingredients in a way no one had ever seen before.

Emeril grabbed fresh Gulf shrimp, spicy Andouille sausage, and an array of vibrant vegetables. He began by sautéing the sausage to release its rich, smoky flavors, then added the shrimp, letting their sweetness meld with the spice. To this, he incorporated bell peppers, onions, and a hint of garlic, creating a colorful and aromatic base. He finished the dish with a touch of homemade Creole seasoning, a splash of white wine, and a garnish of fresh parsley.

As the dish came together, Emeril's kitchen staff watched in awe. Sensing the high stakes of the situation, Emeril knew he needed to keep his team motivated and focused. Channeling his infectious energy, he began to punctuate his movements with a spirited "Bam!" each time he added a key ingredient or seasoning. This not only kept the team engaged but also added a sense of theatricality to the cooking process.

When the dish was finally plated, it was a masterpiece—a vibrant representation of New Orleans cuisine with a Lagasse twist. Emeril personally delivered the plate to the critic, explaining the inspiration and ingredients behind the creation. The critic, initially skeptical, took a bite and was instantly captivated by the bold flavors and innovative combination.

The dish was an overwhelming success, earning rave reviews from the critic and solidifying Emeril Lagasse's reputation as a culinary genius. The incident also marked the birth of "Bam!" as Emeril's signature catchphrase, a symbol of his dynamic cooking style and larger-than-life personality.

This experience not only showcased Emeril's culinary skills but also his ability to think on his feet, innovate under pressure, and inspire those around him. It was a defining moment in his career, paving the way for his future success as a chef, restaurateur, and television personality.

Emeril Lagasse's journey from the kitchens of New Orleans to becoming a household name in the culinary world is a testament to his talent, passion, and indomitable spirit. His story continues to inspire aspiring chefs and food enthusiasts, reminding them that with creativity, confidence, and a touch of flair, they too can create something extraordinary.

The history of the hamburger in America is a tale of innovation and adaptation. One fascinating anecdote traces back to 1904 at the St. Louis World's Fair. Amidst the array of new inventions and foods, a small-time vendor named Fletcher Davis, often referred to as "Old Dave," introduced a novel culinary creation.

Dave, hailing from Athens, Texas, had been serving ground beef patties on bread in his small café for years. His version included mustard, Bermuda onion slices, and pickles, offering a new twist on the traditional steak. When he brought this to the World's Fair, it captured the public's imagination.

The hamburger's journey didn't stop there. In the early 1920s, White Castle, founded by Billy Ingram and Walter Anderson in Wichita, Kansas, standardized the hamburger, ensuring quality and cleanliness, making it an American staple. Their success inspired others, leading to the proliferation of burger joints across the nation.

Thus, from Fletcher Davis's fair booth to the rise of fast-food giants, the hamburger evolved into a symbol of American culture, reflecting the country's ingenuity and love for accessible, delicious food.

The history of pizza delivery in America took a significant leap in the 1960s with the founding of Domino's Pizza. Tom Monaghan and his brother James purchased a small pizza store called DomiNick's in Ypsilanti, Michigan, in 1960. They renamed it Domino's in 1965, and Tom introduced a revolutionary concept: fast, reliable delivery.

Monaghan's vision was to deliver hot, fresh pizza within 30 minutes. To achieve this, he implemented an efficient system, including standardized recipes and streamlined kitchen operations. The promise of quick delivery became Domino's hallmark, famously advertised as the "30 minutes or less" guarantee.

This innovation transformed the pizza industry, making delivery a standard service. Other pizzerias soon followed suit, recognizing the convenience and popularity of having pizza brought straight to customers' doors. By the 1980s, pizza delivery was a common feature in American households, driven by the rise of suburban living and the desire for convenience.

Domino's pioneering efforts not only popularized pizza delivery but also set the stage for the modern food delivery industry, influencing how Americans order and enjoy their meals today.

Random Q & A

Question: Name the Japanese delicacy that can kill you if not prepared properly.

Answer: Fugu.

Fugu is a Japanese dish made from puffer fish. A puffer fish contains a deadly toxin called tetrodotoxin. Each fish contains enough poison to kill 30 people, and there is no known antidote. Japanese chefs obviously must obtain specialized training before being allowed to prepare and serve fugu.

Question: How many licks does it take to get to the center of a Tootsie Pop?

Answer: According to tootsie dot com, there have actually been scientific studies conducted to find this answer, using both human lickers, and machine lickers. Tests indicate it takes between 252 to 411 licks to get to the get inside of a Tootsie Pop. But, if you're like most people, the urge to bite into the pop well before you reach the 252 licks threshold defeats any attempt to count.

Question: In an iconic scene of the movie, *Forrest Gump*, Bubba Blue described to Forrest the different ways he knew to prepare shrimp. How many variations did Bubba mention?

Answer: During the movie *Forrest Gump*, Bubba told Forrest 21 different ways to prepare shrimp, including boiled, fried, and barbecued.

Forrest Gump was released in 1994 and directed by Robert Zemeckis. Zemeckis also directed *Romancing the Stone*, *Back to the Future*, and *The Polar Express*, among others.

Tom Hanks played Forrest Gump, with Robin Wright as Jenny Curran, Sally Field as Ms. Gump, Gary Sinise as Lt. Dan, and Mykelti Williamson as Benjamin Buford "Bubba" Blue.

The young Forrest Gump was played by Michael Conner Humphreys.

Question: During the 1800s what was one of the main sources of meat protein for poor immigrants in New York City?

Answer: Ironically, it was lobster. Prior to the 1900s and beyond, lobster were so plentiful they literally washed ashore around New York City. Poverty stricken immigrants could comb the beach and collect essentially all the lobster they could eat.

Question: Which Italian dish consists of layers of pasta, cheese, and meat sauce?

Answer: Lasagna

Question: Who is the British chef known for the TV show "Hell's Kitchen"?
Answer: Gordon Ramsay

Question: What is the main ingredient in traditional Japanese miso soup?

Answer: Miso paste

Question: What type of wine is made from Pinot Noir grapes?

Answer: Red wine

Question: What is the French term for a culinary chef's workstation?

Answer: Mise en place

Question: Who is the chef behind the famous restaurant Noma in Copenhagen?

Answer: René Redzepi

Question: Which country is the dish paella originally from?

Answer: Spain

Question: What is the main ingredient in guacamole?

Answer: Avocado

Question: Who is the American chef known for popularizing the concept of molecular gastronomy?

Answer: Grant Achatz

Question: What is the primary ingredient in the Italian dessert tiramisu?

Answer: Mascarpone cheese

Question: Which French wine region is known for producing Champagne?

Answer: Champagne region

Question: What type of pasta is shaped like small rice grains and is often used in soups?

Answer: Orzo

Question: Who is the chef and host of the TV show "The French Chef"?

Answer: Julia Child

Question: What is the name of the spicy Korean fermented cabbage dish?

Answer: Kimchi

Question: Which type of wine is traditionally used in making a classic French coq au vin?

Answer: Red wine

Question: Who is the celebrity chef known for his line of cookware and the phrase "Bam!"?

Answer: Emeril Lagasse

Question: What is the main ingredient in hummus?

Answer: Chickpeas

Question: What is the name of the Italian ham that is typically thinly sliced and served uncooked?

Answer: Prosciutto

Question: Who is the chef behind the restaurant "El Bulli" in Spain?

Answer: Ferran Adrià

Question: What is the main ingredient in the dish ratatouille?

Answer: Vegetables

Question: Which wine is made from Riesling grapes?

Answer: White wine

Question: What is the term for a small, savory French pastry filled with a creamy mixture?

Answer: Gougère

Question: Who is the Japanese chef known for his Michelin-starred sushi restaurant in Tokyo?

Answer: Jiro Ono

Question: What is the name of the Indian dish made with chicken marinated in yogurt and spices, then cooked in a tandoor?

Answer: Chicken Tikka

Question: What is the main ingredient in a traditional Greek tzatziki sauce?

Answer: Yogurt

Question: Which type of wine is produced in the Bordeaux region of France?

Answer: Both red and white wine

Question: Who is the chef and television personality known for "Diners, Drive-Ins and Dives"?

Answer: Guy Fieri

Question: What is the name of the classic French dish made of snails cooked in garlic butter?

Answer: Escargot

Question: What is the main ingredient in a Caesar salad dressing?

Answer: Anchovies

Question: Who is the chef known for his "Naked Chef" TV series?

Answer: Jamie Oliver

Question: What is the name of the Spanish cold soup made with tomatoes and other vegetables?

Answer: Gazpacho

Question: What type of wine is traditionally used in the Italian dish risotto?

Answer: White wine

Question: Who is the chef and author known for the book "Kitchen Confidential"?

Answer: Anthony Bourdain

Question: What is the name of the French dish made with duck confit and white beans?

Answer: Cassoulet

Question: What is the main ingredient in the dessert panna cotta?

Answer: Cream

Question: Which type of wine is typically used to make sangria?

Answer: Red wine

Question: Who is the chef behind the restaurant "The French Laundry" in California?

Answer: Thomas Keller

Question: What is the name of the Vietnamese noodle soup that is typically made with beef or chicken?

Answer: Pho

Question: What is the main ingredient in the Japanese dish tempura?

Answer: Battered and deep-fried seafood or vegetables

Question: Which Italian wine region is known for producing Chianti?

Answer: Tuscany

Question: Who is the chef known for the TV show "Good Eats"?

Answer: Alton Brown

Question: What is the name of the Mexican dish made with corn tortillas filled with meat, cheese, and other ingredients?

Answer: Tacos

Question: What is the main ingredient in a traditional French bouillabaisse?

Answer: Fish

Question: Which type of wine is made from Sauvignon Blanc grapes?

Answer: White wine

Question: Who is the chef and television personality known for "Barefoot Contessa"?

Answer: Ina Garten

Question: What is the name of the Thai dish made with stir-fried noodles, eggs, tofu, and peanuts?

Answer: Pad Thai

Question: What is the main ingredient in the Italian dessert cannoli?

Answer: Ricotta cheese

Question: Which wine is typically used to make a classic French Beurre Blanc sauce?

Answer: White wine

Question: Who is the chef behind the restaurant "Momofuku" in New York City?

Answer: David Chang

Question: What is the name of the traditional Japanese rice dish often topped with raw fish?

Answer: Sushi

Question: What is the main ingredient in the Middle Eastern dish falafel?

Answer: Chickpeas or fava beans

Question: Which wine is produced in the Burgundy region of France?

Answer: Both red and white wine

Question: Who is the chef known for the TV show "Iron Chef America"?

Answer: Bobby Flay

Question: What is the name of the Spanish dish made with eggs, potatoes, and onions?

Answer: Tortilla Española

Question: What is the main ingredient in the French dessert crème brûlée?

Answer: Custard

Question: Which type of wine is often used in cooking to deglaze pans and add flavor to dishes?

Answer: White wine

Question: Who is the chef and restaurateur behind "Chez Panisse" in Berkeley, California?

Answer: Alice Waters

Question: What is the name of the Italian dish made with thinly sliced raw meat or fish, typically served as an appetizer?

Answer: Carpaccio

Question: What is the main ingredient in the Indian dish paneer tikka?

Answer: Paneer (Indian cottage cheese)

Business and Finance

President Calvin Coolidge once stated, "The business of America is business."

Coolidge was right. The Gross Domestic Product (GDP)of the United States was $26.9 trillion in 2023.

The GDP of a nation represents the combined market value of all goods and services exchanged during a given year. Economists consider the GDP of a nation the key indicator of its economic health and size. While America has the highest GDP, China comes in second at $17.7 trillion, then Germany at $4.43 trillion, and Japan at $4.23 trillion. From there, the numbers drop to the $2 trillion range with India, UK, France, Italy, Brazil, and Canada leading the world in terms of their respective economies.

Looking at the size of an economy in terms of GDP, the business of America, is business.

But there's more to business and finance than the macro economics of a nation. At the micro level you have individual citizens and small businesses who earn a wage of salary, invest, and borrow money to start a small business or buy a house.

Known for his wit and commonsense, Mark Twain once wrote, "If you owe the bank $100 that's your problem. If you owe the bank $100 million, that's the bank's problem."

While excessive use of abbreviations in business communications may appear unprofessional, or confusing, here are a handful of common abbreviations deemed acceptable.

B2C: Business to Consumer
DSC: Dedicated Short Code
EOD: End of Day
FTFY: Fixed That For You
ICYMI: In Case You Missed It
MMS: Multimedia Messaging Service
SMS: Short Message Service
TLDR: Too Long, didn't Read
TYVM: Thank You Very Much
WIP: Work in Progress
GAAP: Generally Accepted Accounting Principles

The Friday after Thanksgiving has come to be known as Black Friday. This name has nothing to do with race, but is instead a reference to a traditional accounting method of keeping a company's books in red or black ink. Red ink denotes financial losses, and black ink represents profit.

Black Friday is the symbolic day of the year when retail stores could count on transitioning to black ink, and profit, thanks to the Christmas shopping surge. Black Friday is also known for its mob violence, crowds, and out of control shoppers.

The year 2020 put a severe damper on the Black Friday frenzy, and since then, online shopping, and extended sales long before Thanksgiving, have taken the edge off the traditional blockbuster attraction of shopping on Black Friday. But for some people the excitement of shopping and finding a deal remains a draw, prompting tent encampments and long lines in front of popular retail outlets.

Planned obsolescence is a term that refers to a practice of manufacturing products with built-in quality defects that will cause the product to fail within a predictable amount of time, requiring the consumer to replace the item.

The term gained popular usage in the 1950s, but its origins date back to 1924 when Alfred P. Sloan from General Motors developed the concept of redesigning automobiles every year. Prior to this, car manufacturers such as Ford designed an automobile and sold what was essentially the same car year after year. General Motor's shift to annual model changes created a demand among consumers who wanted the latest and best of any product, thus stimulating hyper consumerism we know to this day.

In a similar vein of consumer awareness, caveat emptor is Latin for, "let the buyer beware." In the world of business and consumerism, this puts the onus of any business transaction on the buyer, and serves as a warning to consumers to conduct due diligence prior to parting with their money.

The 1929 Stock Market Crash, often referred to as Black Tuesday, marked the beginning of a decade-long economic downturn known as the Great Depression. This catastrophic event not only wiped out millions of investors but also set off a series of economic calamities that reshaped the global economy and led to widespread financial despair.

During the 1920s, known as the Roaring Twenties, the U.S. experienced significant economic growth and prosperity. The stock market became a symbol of this newfound wealth, with stock prices rising rapidly. Many Americans, including middle-class citizens, invested heavily in the stock market, often buying stocks on margin. Buying on margin meant purchasing stocks with borrowed money, which worked well as long as stock prices continued to rise.

Despite the booming market, there were underlying issues in the economy. Agricultural sectors were struggling due to overproduction and falling prices, and income inequality was widening. Furthermore, industrial production and employment rates began to show signs of slowing down. These issues, however, were largely ignored by investors caught up in the speculative frenzy.

The stock market began to show signs of instability in early September 1929. On October 24, 1929, known as Black Thursday, the market took a significant downturn, with panicked investors selling their stocks in droves. This initial crash was followed by Black Monday and Black Tuesday on October 28 and 29, respectively, where the market lost billions of dollars in value. The Dow Jones Industrial Average fell by almost 25% over those two days.

The crash had an immediate and devastating impact on the American economy. Banks, having invested heavily in the stock market, found themselves on the brink of collapse. As banks failed, people lost their savings, and credit dried up, leading to a decrease in consumer spending and business investment. This created a vicious cycle of declining economic activity.

The stock market crash did not directly cause the Great Depression, but it severely exacerbated the existing economic weaknesses. The subsequent bank failures, reduced consumer spending, and declining industrial output led to widespread unemployment. By 1933, the unemployment rate in the United States had soared to 25%.

The Great Depression was not confined to the United States; it had a global reach. Many European economies, already weakened by the aftermath of World War I, were severely affected. International trade plummeted, leading to further economic decline worldwide. Countries like Germany, which relied on American loans, found themselves in financial turmoil, contributing to the rise of political extremism.

The initial government response to the crisis was inadequate. President Herbert Hoover believed in limited government intervention, advocating for voluntary measures by businesses to maintain employment and wages. However, these measures proved insufficient as the economic situation worsened.

It wasn't until Franklin D. Roosevelt assumed the presidency in 1933 that significant government intervention began. Roosevelt's New Deal programs aimed to provide relief, recovery, and reform. The government launched public works projects, provided financial assistance to the unemployed, and implemented regulations to stabilize the banking system and stock market. While these measures did not end the Great Depression, they helped mitigate some of its worst effects and restored confidence in the economy.

The Great Depression had profound long-term effects on the U.S. and global economies. It led to the establishment of key financial regulations and institutions, such as the Securities and Exchange Commission (SEC) and the Federal Deposit Insurance Corporation (FDIC), aimed at preventing future financial crises. Additionally, the economic hardships and social upheavals of the 1930s significantly influenced political developments worldwide, contributing to the rise of totalitarian regimes and eventually leading to World War II.

The 1929 Stock Market Crash and the ensuing Great Depression were watershed events in economic history. They exposed the vulnerabilities of speculative bubbles and underscored the need for robust financial regulation and government intervention in stabilizing the economy. The lessons learned from this period continue to inform economic policy and financial regulation to this day.

Random Q & A

Question: True or false. Older people are more likely to be victimized by online, email, and telemarketing scams than younger people.

Answer: False. According to a 2021 report from the Federal Trade Commission, younger adults were actually 34 percent more likely to report losing money to fraud compared to those over 60.

Question: What is the largest stock exchange in the world by market capitalization?

Answer: New York Stock Exchange (NYSE)

Question: Who is the founder of Amazon?

Answer: Jeff Bezos

Question: What does the acronym "IPO" stand for in the stock market?

Answer: Initial Public Offering

Question: What is the primary function of the Federal Reserve?

Answer: To regulate the U.S. monetary and financial system

Question: Who is known as the Oracle of Omaha?

Answer: Warren Buffett

Question: What does "REIT" stand for in real estate?

Answer: Real Estate Investment Trust

Question: Which company is known for its slogan "Just Do It"?

Answer: Nike

Question: What does "GDP" stand for in economics?

Answer: Gross Domestic Product

Question: Who founded Microsoft along with Paul Allen?

Answer: Bill Gates

Question: What is the largest commercial bank in the United States by assets?

Answer: JPMorgan Chase

Question: What does the acronym "ETF" stand for in investing?

Answer: Exchange-Traded Fund

Question: Who is the current CEO of Tesla, Inc.?

Answer: Elon Musk

Question: What is the name of the index that tracks the 30 largest publicly traded companies in the U.S.?

Answer: Dow Jones Industrial Average

Question: What is the main purpose of a mutual fund?

Answer: To pool money from many investors to purchase securities

Question: Who is the founder of Facebook?

Answer: Mark Zuckerberg

Question: What does "APR" stand for in finance?

Answer: Annual Percentage Rate

Question: Which company is known for its search engine and advertising platform?

Answer: Google (Alphabet Inc.)

Question: What is the term for a market condition where prices are falling and investor sentiment is pessimistic?

Answer: Bear market

Question: Who is the CEO of Berkshire Hathaway?

Answer: Warren Buffett

Question: What does "FHA" stand for in real estate?

Answer: Federal Housing Administration

Question: What is the largest technology company by revenue as of 2023?

Answer: Apple Inc.

Question: What does the acronym "P/E ratio" stand for?

Answer: Price-to-Earnings ratio

Question: Who founded the Virgin Group?

Answer: Richard Branson

Question: What is the primary purpose of the International Monetary Fund (IMF)?

Answer: To promote global monetary cooperation and financial stability

Question: What is the term for the legal process by which a lender takes possession of a property due to the borrower's failure to make mortgage payments?

Answer: Foreclosure

Question: Who is the CEO of Amazon as of 2023?

Answer: Andy Jassy

Question: What does "NASDAQ" stand for?

Answer: National Association of Securities Dealers Automated Quotations

Question: What is the term for the profit from the sale of an asset or investment?

Answer: Capital gain

Question: Who is the founder of Alibaba Group?

Answer: Jack Ma

Question: What is the name of the index that measures the performance of 500 large companies listed on stock exchanges in the United States?

Answer: S&P 500

Question: What does "FDIC" stand for?

Answer: Federal Deposit Insurance Corporation

Question: Who founded Berkshire Hathaway?

Answer: Oliver Chace (initially as a textile company; Warren Buffett later transformed it into an investment company)

Question: What is the term for the amount by which revenue from sales exceeds costs in a business?

Answer: Profit

Question: Who is the CEO of JPMorgan Chase?

Answer: Jamie Dimon

Question: What is the term for the initial funding needed to start a business?

Answer: Seed capital

Question: Who founded the investment management company Vanguard Group?

Answer: John C. Bogle

Question: What does the acronym "ROI" stand for in finance?

Answer: Return on Investment

Question: What is the term for a market condition where prices are rising and investor sentiment is optimistic?

Answer: Bull market

Question: Who is the CEO of Apple Inc. as of 2023?

Answer: Tim Cook

Question: What does "LIBOR" stand for in banking?

Answer: London Interbank Offered Rate

Question: Who founded the global payment company PayPal?

Answer: Elon Musk, Peter Thiel, and Max Levchin

Question: What is the term for a loan secured by real property through the use of a mortgage note?

Answer: Mortgage

Question: Who is the CEO of Goldman Sachs as of 2023?

Answer: David Solomon

Question: What is the term for the total value of goods and services produced within a country's borders?

Answer: Gross Domestic Product (GDP)

Question: Who founded the company Oracle Corporation?

Answer: Larry Ellison, Bob Miner, and Ed Oates

Question: What does the term "dividend" refer to in investing?

Answer: A payment made by a corporation to its shareholders, usually in the form of cash or additional stock

Question: Who is the CEO of Microsoft as of 2023?

Answer: Satya Nadella

Question: What is the term for the risk of an investment's value decreasing due to economic or market conditions?

Answer: Market risk

Question: Who founded the retail company Walmart?

Answer: Sam Walton

Question: What does "VIX" stand for in the context of stock markets?

Answer: Volatility Index

Question: What is the term for the fixed interest rate at which banks lend to each other overnight?
Answer: Federal funds rate

Question: Who is the CEO of Morgan Stanley as of 2023?

Answer: James Gorman

Question: What is the term for the practice of spreading investments across different asset classes to reduce risk?

Answer: Diversification

Question: Who founded the online payment service Stripe?

Answer: Patrick and John Collison

Question: What does "ESG" stand for in investing?

Answer: Environmental, Social, and Governance

Question: Who is the CEO of Citigroup as of 2023?

Answer: Jane Fraser

Question: What is the term for the market where new securities are issued and sold for the first time?

Answer: Primary market

Question: Who founded the social media platform Twitter?

Answer: Jack Dorsey, Noah Glass, Biz Stone, and Evan Williams

Question: What does "PEST analysis" stand for in business?
Answer: Political, Economic, Social, and Technological analysis

Question: Who is the CEO of Bank of America as of 2023?

Answer: Brian Moynihan

Random Questions and Answers

What's a random walk down trivia lane without a collection of random questions and answers?

In the tradition of a pub trivia contest, here's a double fistful of random questions you may encounter at your next trivia tournament.

Question: Name the top 10 most popular television shows of all time.

Answer: According to *Rolling Stone* magazine, The Mary Tyler Moore Show, Atlanta, Cheers, Mad Men, Seinfeld, Fleabag, The Wire, Breaking Bad, The Simpsons, and The Sopranos.

In the UK, some of the most popular and uniquely British television shows include Fawlty Towers, Doctor Who, Mr. Bean, Planet Earth, and Peaky Blinders.

Question: What three United States presidents died on the 4th of July?

Answer: John Adams, Thomas Jefferson, and James Monroe. Adams and Jefferson both died in 1826. Monroe died in 1831.

Question: What is the doll Barbie's full name?

Answer: According to barbiemedia.com, Barbie was born on 9 March 1959, the date she was first put on pubic display at the New York Toy Fair. According to her creators, Barbie's full name is Barbara Millicent Roberts. She is from Willows, Wisconsin. Truly, an All-American girl with a taste for nice things.

Question: What is the the name the ancient Greeks gave to the god of war?

Answer: Ares is the Greek god of war and courage, and the mythological son of Zeus and Hera. The ancient Romans called their god of war Mars. He is the mythological son of Jupiter and Juno.

Question: According to online historical records regarding the search engine Google, a *googol* is the number 1, followed by 100 zeroes. A big number, indeed. Prior to calling the search engine site Google, what was Google's original name?

Answer: Apparently, *Backrub*. Thankfully, the founders of Google did not stick with that. Could you imagine, billions of people per day would be visualizing back rubs every time they searched online for a biscuit recipe or funny cat video..

Question: Some world records were made to be broken, such as swimming the fastest 100 meter butterfly, or eating the most hot dogs in under 90 seconds. But others remain unchallenged, due to their sheer oddity.

For example, did you know there's a record for the longest time spent twirling a hula hoop while under water? Or, the furthest distance spent riding a bicycle while balancing a milk jug on one's head?

Name the eccentric who holds the record for the most world records?

Answer: Ashrita Furman gained fame and notoriety by setting world records for things other people never thought of. According to the purveyors of all things worthy of recording, *The Guinness Book of World Records*, Furman set 600 records, 200 of which are still standing.

By the way, *The Guinness Book of World Records* was first published in 1955. The book is an annual, published by the Jim Pattison Group in London. The book is a veritable goldmine for trivia buffs.

Question: There is one place in America where you can stand and have your feet in four states simultaneously. This place is appropriately called, Four Corners. What four states meet at Four Corners?

Answer: Utah, Colorado, Arizona and New Mexico.

Question: What is the most commonly misspelled word in the English language?

Answer: Accommodate takes the cake for difficulty, according to how often it is misspelled by people consulting dictionary dot com and thesaurus dot com. Linguists claim words with double consonants are the most often misspelled. The top 10 most commonly misspelled words in English include: acquit, cemetery, exhilarated, hierarchy, inoculate, liaison, memento, pastime, pronunciation, and vacuum.

Personally, the word "Sheriff" often trips me up. I can never remember if it's two Rs or two Fs.

Question: It's hard to believe there was a time when people did not order food "to-go," or drive with one hand while texting and holding a hamburger with the other, but in the 1700s the concept of a "sandwich" did not exist, until an avid gambler decided he was tired of leaving the gambling tables to eat and ordered his butler to throw his meal between two slices of bread and hand it to him. Thus was born the sandwich. What is the name of the gambler who invented the sandwich?

Answer: The Earl of Sandwich, John Montagu.

Question: In ancient Greek mythology, what is the name of the sky and thunder god, who rules on Mount Olympus as king of the gods?

Answer: Zeus is king of the gods in ancient Greek mythology. His Roman equivalent is called Jupiter.

Question: How many bones are there in the human body?

Answer: There are 206 bones in the human body. The largest bone in the human body is the upper leg bone called the femur, and the smallest is the stapes, tucked inside the inner ear.

Question: An American named Robert Wadlow is believed to be the tallest man who ever lived. He died in 1940 at the age of 22 due to an enlarged pituitary gland. Was he 7, 8, or 9 feet tall?

Answer: Wadlow was just under 9 feet tall at 8 feet 11 inches. It's not known whether he ever tried to fit into an airplane seat or not.

Question: The board game, Monopoly, is a popular game that requires players to acquire real estate to defeat the other players. What year was Monopoly first sold to the public, and what toy manufacturer owns the rights to the game to this day?

Answer: A woman named Elizabeth Magie invented the game of Monopoly in 1902. It was patented in 1904 under the name, The Landlord's Game. Parker Brothers refined the game and began selling it in 1933, using the name, Monopoly.

Parker Brothers introduced the game of Monopoly to the world on

Question: Which planet in our solar system is known as the "Red Planet"?

Answer: Mars.

Question: What is the chemical symbol for gold?

Answer: Au.

Question: Who painted the famous artwork "Starry Night"?

Answer: Vincent van Gogh.

Question: What is the capital city of Australia?

Answer: Canberra.

Question: Which country is famous for producing the most coffee in the world?

Answer: Brazil.

Question: What is the main ingredient in guacamole?

Answer: Avocado.

Question: What is the chemical symbol for water?

Answer: H_2O. Water is comprised of hydrogen and oxygen. While humans breathe oxygen to live, the Earth's atmosphere is actually 78 percent nitrogen and 21 percent oxygen.

Question: Which river is the longest in the world?

Answer: The Nile River.

Question: What is the name of the tower in Italy known for its leaning angle?

Answer: The Leaning Tower of Pisa.

Question: In which year did the Titanic sink?

Answer: 1912.

Question: What is the capital of Canada?

Answer: Ottawa.

Question: What is the tallest mountain in the world?

Answer: Mount Everest, at 29,031 feet.

Question: What is the largest ocean on Earth?

Answer: The Pacific Ocean, at 60 million square miles. The Atlantic has 41 million square miles.

Question: Who is known as the father of modern physics?

Answer: Albert Einstein.

Question: Which famous scientist formulated the three laws of motion?

Answer: Isaac Newton.

In Newton's First Law, Newton theorized that a body in motion remains in motion unless an outside force interferes, and that a body at rest remains at rest unless acted upon by an outside force. For example, in a game of billiards a ball remains at rest on the table until another ball hits it. Likewise, a ball in motion on the table remains in motion until contact with another ball, the bumpers, or gravity interrupts its movement.

Newton's Second Law states the force or energy of an object in motion is equal to its mass and speed. Ironically, this closely resemble Einstein's Theory of Relativity, E=MC squared. In practical terms, if you've ever witnessed an accident between two vehicles, you may have noticed the smaller vehicle takes the brunt of the impact. This is because the mass and speed of the vehicles dictates the energy of the vehicles, meaning the heavier vehicle delivers more energy at point of impact.

Newton's Third Law in every action, there is always opposed an equal reaction. Back on the billiards table, when two balls collide, the repel each other in opposite directions. Astronauts learned about the Third Law when they attempted to make repairs to their spacecraft in a zero gravity environment. The simple turning of a wrench would put their bodies in a spin, unless they were anchored to the ship, which even then exerted force on the spaceship itself.

Question: What is the chemical symbol for iron?

Answer: Fe.

Question: In Greek mythology, who is the goddess of wisdom and warfare?

Answer: Athena.

Question: What is the name of the mythological Greek woman immortalized by Christopher Marlowe as the "face that launched a thousand ships?"

Answer: Helen of Troy. Her abduction by Paris, mythological Prince of Troy, led to the Trojan War.

Question: What is a doppelganger?

Answer: Doppelganger is a German word meaning "double goer." In popular usage, it refers to a person who looks just like yourself. President Abraham Lincoln reported seeing a doppelganger in a mirror, which his spiritually inclined wife, Mary Todd Lincoln, interpreted as a bad omen. Shortly after seeing his doppelganger America was plunged into a civil war, and of course, his assassination by John Wilkes Booth on 14 April 1865.

Question: In a website browser address bar, what do the the three letters, www, stand for?

Answer: World Wide Web. The online network of computers and databases from around the world that we know of as the Internet was first created in 1969 when defense contractors and various scientists devised a way to network computers and share access to mainframes under the Defense Advanced Research Projects Agency (DARPA). This early network came to be known as ARPANET.

Progress takes time, however, so it was not until 1989 that consumers first heard the AOL greeting, "Welcome, you've got mail."

The voice on the America Online (AOL) trademarked web browsing software was a man named Elwood Edwards. He used a home cassette recorder to create four simple words or phrases: Welcome. You've got mail. File's done. Goodbye.

Question: Speaking of mail, what actress played opposite of Tom Hanks in the 1998 film, *You've Got Mail*?

Answer: Meg Ryan.

The *You've Got Mail* romantic comedy was based on a 1940 movie called *The Shop Around the Corner*. This film was in turn inspired by a 1937 Hungarian play, which drew its inspiration from Jane Austen's classic romance *Pride and Prejudice*, written in 1813. Thank you, Ms. Austen.

During the movie *You've Got Mail*, Meg Ryan is infatuated with a book she recommends to her unknown (Tom Hanks) online pen pal. The book, *Pride and Prejudice*, of course.

Towards the end of the film when Meg Rayan is visiting the children's section of the Fox Books bookstore, she helps the store clerk with a book title a struggling customer was trying to find. The book was *Ballet Shoes* by Noel Streatfield, one of the most popular books in a series created by the author.

www.ingramcontent.com/pod-product-compliance
Lightning Source LLC
Chambersburg PA
CBHW070825250726
48662CB00003B/1088